The BIG BOOK of LOGOS

Edited by
David E. Carter

Book Design
Suzanna M.W. Brown

Production & Layout
Kristin J. Back

The Big Book of Logos

First published 1999 by Hearst Books International
1350 Avenue of the Americas
New York, NY 10019

ISBN: 0-688-16815-9

Distributed in the U.S. and Canada by
Watson-Guptill Publications
1515 Broadway
New York, NY 10036
Tel: (800) 451-1741
          (732) 363-4511 in NJ, AK, HI
Fax: (732) 363-0338

Distributed throughout the rest of the world by
Hearst Books International
1350 Avenue of the Americas
New York, NY 10019
Fax: (212) 261-6795

First Published in Germany by
Nippan
Nippon Shuppan Ilanbai
Deutschland GmbH
D-40549 Dusseldorf
Telephone: (0211) 504 8089
Fax: (0211) 504 9326

ISBN: 3-931884-45-7

Printed in Hong Kong by Everbest Printing Company
through Four Colour Imports, Louisville, Kentucky.

It was a dark and stormy night.

The publisher had said, "How about doing a big book of logos—almost 400 pages, with the book in full color?"

As lightning flashed outside in the woods, casting flickering shadows on the parlor wall, David Carter paced the Persian carpet wondering how to go about gathering materials for such a book.

Suddenly, inspiration came. "We'll call the book LOGO 2000," Carter thought. Soon, designers from all over America were invited to send their best work.

More than 11,000 logos came in to be considered. After a long process of elimination, approximately 2,500 logos were chosen for this book.

And somewhere along the way, the title became **The Big Book of Logos**.

It's an appropriate title, since this is the largest logo book ever published in America.

This big book shows some of the best logo design work in America, as nearly every top design firm in the country submitted work for the book.

This comprehensive book should become a classic reference source, as designers can flip the pages and see a huge variety of styles and techniques for logo creation.

1.

2.

3.

4.

5.

6.

7.

8.

9.

10.

11.

12.

13.

14.

15.

16.

17.

18.

19.

(all)

Design Firm **Lippincott & Margulies**

1.
Client   *Abbott*
2.
Client   *Allied Corporation*
3.
Client   *Amtrak*
Designer   J. Gordon Lippincott
4.
Client   *Guidant*
5.
Client   *Harris Bank*
Designer   Kenneth Love
6.
Client   *Bank Atlantic*
7.
Client   *Harvard Vanguard*
Designers   Jerry Kuyper, Brendán Murphy
8.
Client   *American Greetings*
Designers   Arthur Congdon, Jack Weller

9.
Client   *Handok*
Designer   Kenneth Love
10.
Client   *UNUM*
11.
Client   *Hartmarx*
12.
Client   *Primerica*
13.
Client   *Kobrick Cendant Funds*
Designers   Kenneth Love, Brendán Murphy
14.
Client   *Caltex*
15.
Client   *Comerica*
16.
Client   *Samsung*
Designer   Constance Birdsall
17.
Client   *The Gillette Company*
Designer   Constance Birdsall
18.
Client   *Finova*
Designer   Constance Birdsall
19.
Client   *Roadway "caliber"*
Designer   Kenneth Love

1.  FMC

2. Scripps

3.  TELUS

4. SOUTHERN COMPANY

5. Continental

6. PRAXAIR

7. DOMAIN ENERGY

8. DIMON

9.  TENNECO

10. SCANA

11.

12.

13.

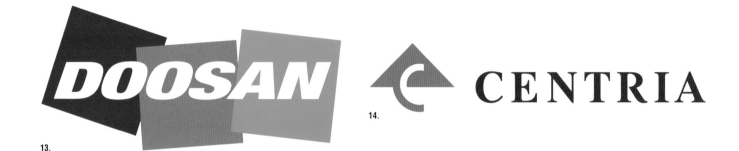

14.

15.

16.

17.

18.

19.

(all)

Design Firm **Lippincott & Margulies**

1.
Client   *FMC*

2.
Client   *Scripps*
Designers   Jerry Kuyper, Brendán Murphy

3.
Client   *Telus*
Designer   Kenneth Love

4.
Client   *Southern Company*
Designer   Constance Birdsall

5.
Client   *Continental Airlines*
Designer   Constance Birdsall

6.
Client   *Praxair*

7.
Client   *Domain Energy (Tenneco)*
Designer   Ken Love

8.
Client   *Dimon*
Designer   Ken Love

9.
Client   *Tenneco*
Designer   Kenneth Love

10.
Client   *Scana*

11.
Client   *Nynex*

12.
Client   *Baskin Robbins*

13.
Client   *Doosan*
Designers   Kenneth Love, Alex de Jánosi

14.
Client   *Centria (Smith Steelite)*
Designer   Jerry Kuyper

15.
Client   *United Technologies*

16.
Client   *Travelers Group*
Designer   Constance Birdsall

17.
Client   *Conoco "breakplace"*

18.
Client   *The St. Paul*

19.
Client   *Sonic*
Designer   Kenneth Love

1. INFINITI

2.

3. *dyneon*
A 3M•HOECHST ENTERPRISE

4. **conectiv**

5.

6. THE FITNESS CENTER OF EXCELLENCE

7.

8.

9.

NITROMED

10.

ENRON CORP

11.

The McGraw·Hill Companies

12.

Pizza Hut

13.

ALSA

14.

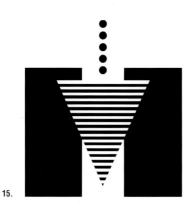

15.

1, 3, 4, 5, 11, 12, 13
Design Firm **Lippincott & Margulies**
2, 7-10, 14, 15
Design Firm **TGD Communications, Inc.**
6
Design Firm **Ted DeCagna Graphic Design**
1.
Client   *Infiniti*
2.
Client   *Borello White Printing*
Designers   Rochelle Gray, Catherine Conley
3.
Client   *Dyneon*
Designer   Rodney Abbot
4.
Client   *Conectiv (Delmarva Power)*
Designer   Constance Birdsall
5.
Client   *PPG*
6.
Client   *American Standard Corporation*
Designer   Ted DeCagna (Choice Signs)

7.
Client   *National Health Strategies*
Designers   Rochelle Gray, Eva Barsin
8.
Client   *Alexandria Chamber of Commerce*
Designers   Rochelle Gray, Leonardo Bentos
9.
Client   *Alexandra Doctor's Network*
Designers   Rochelle Gray, Trish Palasik
10.
Client   *Euromed*
Designer   Chip Griffin
11.
Client   Enron Corporation
12.
Client   The McGraw-Hill Companies
Designer   Constance Birdsall
13.
Client   *Pizza Hut*
14.
Client   *Analytical Life Science Systems Association*
Designers   Chris Harrison, Gloria Vestal
15.
Client   *Minkoff Corporation*
Designer   Rochelle Gray

1.

2.

3.

4.

5.

6.

7.

8.

9.

1, 3 - 7
Design Firm **Lippincott & Margulies**

2.
Design Firm **FRCH Design Worldwide (Cincinnati)**

8
Design Firm **Pentagram Design, Inc.**

9
Design Firm **Bob Rankin Design**

1.
Client   EATON

2.
Client   Harrah's (Carnaval Court)
Designers   Eric Daniel, Gina Beckerink

3.
Client   Humana

4.
Client   Fraser Papers
Designer   Jerry Kuyper

5.
Client   Experian (TRW)
Designer   Alex de Jánosi

6.
Client   Humana
Designers   Jerry Kuyper, Brendán Murphy

7.
Client   Flagstar
Designer   Constance Birdsall

8.
Client   Successmaker Solo
Designers   Lowell Williams, Bill Carson

9.
Client   Move It
Designer   Bob Rankin
(opposite)
Client   University Mall
Design Firm **FRCH Design Worldwide (Cincinnati)**
Designers   Juliette Fiehrer, Erik Brown

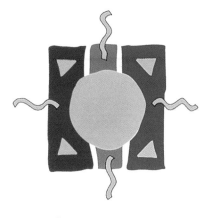

university
mall

▼

11

1.

Van Romer Chiropractic

2.

3.

4.

5.

GENEVA, NY
SENSATIONAL BY NATURE!

6.

7.

8.

9.

10.

11.

12.

13.

14.

15.

1, 4, 5, 8, 10, 11, 14, 15		**8.**	
Design Firm **Mickelson Design & Assoc.**		Client	*Story Time*
2, 3, 6, 7, 12		Designer	Alan Mickelson
Design Firm **In House Graphic Design, Inc.**		**9.**	
9, 13		Client	*Challenge International*
Design Firm **Lightspeed Commercial Arts**		Designer	Michael J. Hamers
1.		**10.**	
Client	*Scheaffer Collection Agency*	Client	*Cedar Rapids Recreation Commission*
Designer	Alan Mickelson	Designers	Mary Bendgen, Alan Mickelson
2.		**11.**	
Client	*Van Romer Chiropractic*	Client	*Cedar Rapids Recreation Commission*
Designer	Dennis Angelo	Designers	Mary Bendgen, Alan Mickelson
3.		**12.**	
Client	*In House Graphic Design, Inc.*	Client	*Morley Financial Services*
Designer	Dennis Angelo	Designer	Dennis Angelo
4.		**13.**	
Client	*Tunes & Tones*	Client	*Institute for Change Research*
Designer	Alan Mickelson	Designer	Michael J. Hamers
5.		**14.**	
Client	*Harmony Business Machines*	Client	*Cedar Rapids Recreation Commission*
Designer	Alan Mickelson	Designers	Mary Bendgen, Alan Mickelson
6.		**15.**	
Client	*Geneva Area Chamber of Commerce*	Client	*Professional Reclamation Inc.*
Designer	Dennis Angelo	Designer	Alan Mickelson
7.			
Client	*Mobilnet Management Services, Inc.*		
Designer	Dennis Angelo		

1.

2.

3.

4.

5.

6.

GLEN BURNIE MALL

7.

1 - 7
Design Firm **Kiku Obata & Company**
1.
Client   *St. Louis Public Schools*
Designer   Jeanna Stoll
2.
Client   *Great Lakes Science Center*
Designer   Kathleen Robert
3.
Client   *Zaro's Bread Basket*
Designer   Joe Floresca
4.
Client   *City of Wildwood, MO*
Designer   Amy Knopf

5.
Client   *Coors Field*
Designer   Todd Mayberry
6.
Client   *Bluefins*
Designer   Kathleen Robert
7.
Client   *Simon DeBartolo Group*
Designer   Todd Mayberry
(opposite)
Client   *Aronoff Center for the Arts*
Design Firm **FRCH Design Worldwide (Cincinnati)**
Designers   Michael Beeghly, Martin Treu, Eric Daniel

1.

2.

3.

4.

5.

6.

ErgoCentrics, Inc.

7.

8.

9.

10.

11.

12.

13.

ROCK AND ROLL
HALL OF FAME + MUSEUM

14.

15.

16.

1, 10, 14, 16		**8.**	
Design Firm **Nesnadny + Schwartz**		Client	*Minneapolis Institute of Arts*
2 - 8, 12		Designer	Bruce Edwards
Design Firm **Rapp Collins Communications**		**9.**	
9, 11, 13		Client	*Roto-Rooter*
Design Firm **Kiku Obata & Company**		Designers	Jim Datema, Rich Nelson
15		**10.**	
Design Firm **Pentagram Design, Inc.**		Client	*The GlobalServe Corporation*
1.		Designer	Gregory Oznowich
Client	*Hanna Perkins*	**11.**	
Designers	Michelle Moehler, Melissa Petrollini	Client	*Juice & Joe*
2.		Designer	Liz Sullivan
Client	*Timber Creek*	**12.**	
Designer	Bruce Edwards	Client	*Minnetonka Center for the Arts*
3.		Designer	Yves Roux
Client	*Rowdy Boards*	**13.**	
Designers	Yves Roux, Floyd Sipe	Client	*Ameren Corporation*
4.		Designer	Scott Gericke
Client	*Salon et Soleil*	**14.**	
Designer	Bruce Edwards	Client	*Rock and Roll Hall of Fame and Museum*
5.		Designers	Joyce Nesnadny, Michelle Moehler, Timothy Lachina, Brian Lavy, Mark Schwartz
Client	*Kenn Ingalls*		
Designer	Ed Hernandez	**15.**	
6.		Client	*Zoological Society of Houston*
Client	*ErgoCentrics*	Designers	Lowell Williams, Bill Carson
Designer	Floyd Sipe	**16.**	
7.		Client	*Fortran Printing, Inc.*
Client	*Kathryn Beich—division of Nestlé*	Designer	Joyce Nesnadny
Designer	Bruce Edwards		

17

BEAVER COLLEGE

THE
COMMON
THREAD

1.

coaches vs cancer

2.

HResu!ts®

3.

Cricket Hill

4.

Doylestown Presbyterian Church

5.

BIRDY

6.

PERFORMING ARTS LEAGUE of PHILADELPHIA

7.

1 - 7
Design Firm **Art 270, Inc.**
1.
Client   *Beaver College*
Designer   John Opet
2.
Client   *Coaches vs. Cancer*
Designer   Dana Sykes
3.
Client   *HResults!*
Designer   Steve Kuttruff
4.
Client   *Cricket Hill Estate*
Designer   Steve Kuttruff

5.
Client   *Doylestown Presbyterian Church*
Designers   Pat Singer, Carl Mill
6.
Client   *Philadelphia Theatre Company*
Designer   Steve Kuttruff
7.
Client   *The Performing Arts League
            of Philadelphia*
Designer   Pat Singer
(opposite)
Client   *Aca Joe*
Design Firm **FRCH Design Worldwide
            (Cincinnati)**
Designers   Tim Frame, Bob Swank

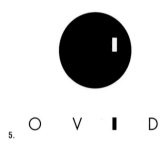

1.

2. **x** a n d **o**

3.

4.

O V **I** D

5.

6.

7.

8.

9.

10.

11.

12.

B A S E B A L L

13.

L E X A N T™

The Power of Health

14.

Mickey on line

15.

16.

17.

1, 3, 4, 6, 7, 15, 17
Design Firm **Yoe! Studio**
2, 5, 8, 11, 14
Design Firm **The Leonhardt Group**
9, 10
Design Firm **Pentagram Design, Inc.**
12
Design Firm **Love Packaging Group**
13, 16
Design Firm **Louis London**

1.
Client   *Miller Brewing Co.*
Designer   Craig Yoe
2.
Client   *Xando*
Designer   Candace Morgan
3.
Client   *Jim Henson Productions*
Designer   Craig Yoe
4.
Client   *3-D Inc.*
Designers   Yoe! Studio
5.
Client   *Ovid Technologies*
Designers   Ray Ueno, Dennis Clouse
6.
Client   *Matinee*
Designers   Yoe! Studio
7.
Client   *Parachute Press*
Designers   Yoe! Studio
8.
Client   *Gargoyles Eyewear*
Designers   Mark Popich, Greg Morgan

9.
Client   *Taco Bueno*
Designers   Lowell Williams, Bill Carson,
Jeff Williams, Julie Hoyt,
Marc Stephens
10.
Client   *Thomas Hayward*
Designers   Lowell Williams, Bill Carson
11.
Client   *Experience Music Project*
Designers   Candace Morgan, Ray Ueno,
Steve Watson, Renee Sullivan,
Greg Morgan
12.
Client   *The Fantastic World of
Gourmet Chocolate*
Designers   Chris West, Brian Miller
13.
Client   *Kirkwood Athletic Assoc.*
Art Director   David Bannecke
14.
Client   *Lexant*
Designer   Janee Kreinheder
15.
Client   *Mickey & Co.*
Designers   Yoe! Studio
16.
Client   *Shell Oil Company*
Art Director   Sam Monica
17.
Client   *Parachute Press*
Designers   Yoe! Studio

1. **S P G**

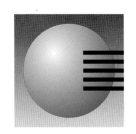

2. ADVANCED LASER GRAPHICS

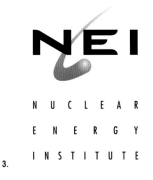

NEI

NUCLEAR

ENERGY

INSTITUTE

3.

4.

GCSS ARMY

Global Combat Support System–Army

5.

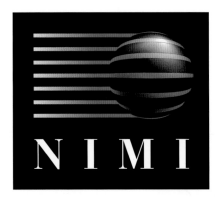

NIMI

6.

O | D | C

7.

1 - 7
Design Firm **Tim Kenney Design Partners**

1.
Client   *Solutions Planning Group*
Designers   Tim Kenney, Tom Snoreck

2.
Client   *Advanced Laser Graphics*
Designer   Tim Kenney

3.
Client   *Nuclear Energy Institute*
Designers   Tim Kenney, Tom Snoreck

4.
Client   *Global Cable Consulting Group*
Designers   Tim Kenney, Monica Banko

5.
Client   *GRC International, Inc.*
Designers   Tim Kenney, Moira Ratchford

6.
Client   *NASDAQ International Market Initiatives (NIMI)*
Designers   Tim Kenney, Moira Ratchford

7.
Client   *Overseas Development Council*
Designer   Tim Kenney

(opposite)
Client   *Chesapeake Bagel—St. Louis*
Design Firm   **Kiku Obata & Company**
Designer   Jane McNeely

1.

2.

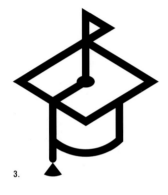

3.

AMC

THE WORLD'S LARGEST
TRADE MART/TRADE SHOW
ORGANIZATION

4.

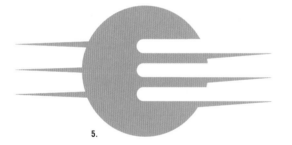

5.

6.

CONCORD
MALL

7.

8.

9.

10.

11.

12.

13.

14. AmeriHealth

15.

1 - 3, 6 - 9, 12, 13, 15
   Design Firm **Joseph Rattan Design**
4, 5, 10, 11, 14
   Design Firm **Young & Martin Design**

1.
Client	*Object Space*
Designer	Joseph Rattan

2.
Client	*Batrus Hollweg*
Designer	Joseph Rattan

3.
Client	*Benton Shipp Golf Tournament*
Designer	Joseph Rattan

4.
Client	*AMC, Inc.*
Designers	Steve Martin, Joe Alcober

5.
Client	*EPTI*
Designer	Steve Martin

6.
Client	*Friends of WRR*
Designer	Joseph Rattan

7.
Client	*Concord Mall*
Designer	Diana McKnight

8.
Client	*Habitat for Humanity*
Designers	Joseph Rattan, Greg Morgan

9.
Client	*Hanaco*
Designer	Joseph Rattan

10.
Client	*Global Trade Partners*
Designers	Ed Young, Steve Martin

11.
Client	*Wesli Mancini Fabric Design*
Designer	Steve Martin

12.
Client	*International Broadcast Systems, Inc.*
Designer	Joseph Rattan

13.
Client	*Cintron Lehner Barrett*
Designer	Joseph Rattan

14.
Client	*AmeriHealth*
Designer	Steve Martin

15.
Client	*Group Gallagher*
Designers	Joseph Rattan, Greg Morgan

25

1. S O N G S M I T H

2.

version X

3.

A S C E N T

4.

G A T E W A Y

5.

Williams Construction **6.**

7.

1, 6
Design Firm **Lauren Smith Design**
2, 4, 5, 7
Design Firm **The Graphic Expression, Inc.**
3
Design Firm **Glyphix Studio**
1.
  Client   *Songsmith*
  Designer Lauren Smith
2.
  Client   *Aquatic Leisure International*
  Designer Kurt Finkbeiner
3.
  Client   *Version X*
  Designer Brad Wilder
4.
  Client   *Ascent Entertainment Group*
  Designer Kurt Finkbeiner

5.
  Client   *Gateway Insurance Company*
  Designer Kurt Finkbeiner
6.
  Client   *Williams Construction*
  Designer Lauren Smith
7.
  Client   *Young at Art*
  Designer Kurt Finkbeiner
(opposite)
  Client   *Dayton Mall*
  Design Firm **FRCH Design Worldwide—**
            (Cincinnati)
  Designer Michael Beeghly, Charles Aenlle,
            Erik Brown, Lori Seibert

DAYTON MALL

1.

GRAPHIC PIZZA

2. William Morrow and Associates

Avante

3.

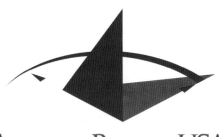

ANNUITY BUYERS USA

4.

FARMLAND MORTGAGE

5.

artax

6.

7.

8. American Air Show Network

ST. JOHN'S
ORTHOPÆDIC
SERVICES

9.

10.

Crest Graphics, Inc. 11.

Building B Creations

12.

13.

DANet

14.

ESPRIT

DOMESTIQUE ET
INTERNAÇIONALE

15.

2 - 15
Design Firm **Glyphix Studio**
1.
  Client   *Graphic Pizza*
  Designer   Brad Wilder
2.
  Client   *William Morrow & Assoc.*
  Designer   Brad Wilder
3.
  Client   *Avante*
  Designer   Brad Wilder
4.
  Client   *Annuity Buyers, USA*
  Designer   Paul Ruettgers
5.
  Client   *Farmland Mortgage*
  Designer   Brad Wilder
6.
  Client   *Artax*
  Designer   Brad Wilder
7.
  Client   *Glyphix Studio*
  Designer   Brad Wilder

8.
  Client   *American Airshow Network*
  Designer   Brad Wilder
9.
  Client   *St. John's Orthopaedic Services*
  Designer   Brad Wilder
10.
  Client   *US Tel*
  Designer   Brad Wilder
11.
  Client   *Crest Graphics, Inc.*
  Designer   Brad Wilder
12.
  Client   *Building B Creations*
  Designer   Brad Wilder
13.
  Client   *Equibond*
  Designer   Brad Wilder
14.
  Client   *Danet*
  Designer   Brad Wilder
15.
  Client   *Esprit*
  Designer   Brad Wilder

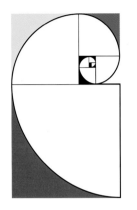

1.

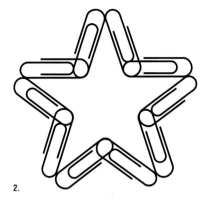

2.

3.

4.

5.

6.

7.

1, 6
Design Firm **DesignLab**
2 - 5, 7
Design Firm **Michael Lee Advertising & Design, Inc.**
1.
Client *GSH Design*
Designers Kennah Harcum, Gary Henley
2.
Client *Texas Office Products*
Designer Michael Lee
3.
Client *SeaSea Multi-Hulls*
Designers Michael Lee, Debby Stasinopoulou
4.
Client *St. Elizabeth Hospital's Wilton P. Hebert Health & Wellness Center*
Designers Michael Lee, Debby Stasinopoulou

5.
Client *Lamar University*
Designer Michael Lee
6.
Client *DesignLab*
Designer Kennah Harcum
7.
Client *XL Systems*
Designers Michael Lee, Debby Stasinopoulou
(opposite)
Client *Harrah's (OnStage)*
Design Firm **FRCH Design Worldwide— (Cincinnati)**
Designers Paul Lechleiter, Steve McGowan, Eric Daniel

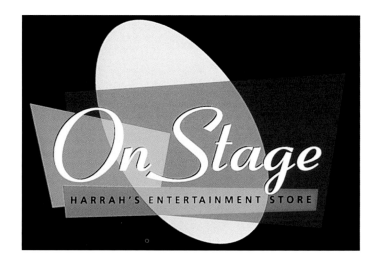

1.

2.

3.

4.

5.

6. SHADOW WOOD

7. Rutenberg Homes

8.

PEGASUS
TRAVEL
9.

10.

meadowlark

11.

12.

13.

14.

15.

(all)		
Design Firm	**The Brothers Bogusky**	
Designer	Bill Bogusky	
1.		
Client	Pan American Bank	
2.		
Client	Raintree Homes	
3.		
Client	Ville La Reine	
4.		
Client	Diabetes Research Institute	
5.		
Client	Miacord	
6.		
Client	Shadow Wood	
7.		
Client	Rutenberg Homes	

8.	
Client	Deep 6
9.	
Client	Pegasus Travel
10.	
Client	Art Center
11.	
Client	Meadowlark Estates
12.	
Client	TransAmerica
13.	
Client	Robinson Racing Products
14.	
Client	Hydrotech
15.	
Client	University Federal Savings & Loan

1.

LINDA
CREED
Breast Cancer
2. Foundation

STRATEGIC FOCUS
3. C O N S U L T I N G

4.

5.

6.

BAR FOUNDATION

7. LEGACY SOCIETY

asterisk

8.

1-8
Design Firm **Art 270, Inc.**
1.
Client   *Abington Hospital*
Designers   Pat Singer, Carl Mill
2.
Client   *Linda Creed Breast Cancer Foundation*
Designers   Steve Kutruff, Sue Ströhm
3.
Client   *Strategic Focus Consulting*
Designers   Carl Mill
4.
Client   *State Street Cafe*
Designers   Dana Sykes, Carl Mill
5.
Client   *CVB Consultants*
Designer   Carl Mill

6.
Client   *Interconnect Systems, Inc.*
Designer   Carl Mill
7.
Client   *Philadelphia Bar Foundation Legal Society*
Designers   Dianne Mill, Pat Singer, Sue Ströhm, Dana Breslin
8.
Client   *Asterisk*
Designer   Carl Mill
(opposite)
Client   *The Minnesota Zoo*
Design Firm **Rapp Collins Communications**
Designer   Bruce Edwards

SOUTHWEST GOURMET
F O O D   S H O W

1.

THE RIVER WALK SAN ANTONIO

2.

alamo.com

3.

4.

5.

WE SUPPORT WORLDS

6.

splash
down™

7.

Central Park Mall

8.

9.

10.

11.

12.

13.

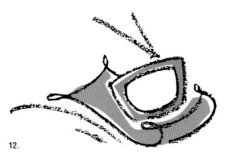

14.

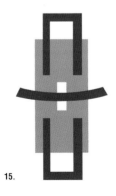

15.

1 - 11
Design Firm **Creative Link Studio, Inc.**
12 - 14
Design Firm **Nestor•Stermole Visual Communication Group**
15
Design Firm **Crimm Design**

1.
Client *Central Park Mall Southwest Gourmet Food Show*
Designers Kyle Derr, Kevin La Rue
2.
Client *Riverwalk San Antonio Video*
Designer Mark Broderick
3.
Client *Alamo.com*
Designers Drew Dela Cruz, Kyle Derr
4.
Client *Pacificare Matters on Maternity*
Designer Mark Broderick
5.
Client *Racquetball and Fitness Clubs Kidzone*
Designers Kevin La Rue, Kyle Derr, Mark Broderick
6.
Client *Origin Software*
Designers Kevin La Rue, Mark Broderick, Kyle Derr

7.
Client *Coca-Cola Southwest— Splash Down*
8.
Client *Central Park Mall*
Designers Kevin La Rue, Cheryl Abts
9.
Client *Universal Advisory Services, Inc.*
Designers Mark Broderick, Kyle Derr, Kevin La Rue
10.
Client *San Antonio Parks & Recreation JazzSalive*
Designer Mark Broderick
11.
Client *San Antonio Sports Foundation*
Designers Kyle Derr, Kevin La Rue
12.
Client *Tapestry International*
Designers Okey Nester, Jeanne Grecco
13.
Client *Millenium Pharmaceuticals*
Designers Okey Nestor, Carla Miller
14.
Client *Wolper Sales Agency*
Designer Okey Nestor
15.
Client *Crimm Design*
Designer G.M. Crimm

1.

PLS

2.

NTCA

The Voice of Rural Telecommunications

3.

4.

5.

ACCA
SOURCE

6.

7. OPASTCO

1, 4, 5
Design Firm **Frank D'Astolfo Design**
2, 3, 6, 7
Design Firm **Coleman Design Group, Inc.**
1.
Client *Alimenterics Inc.*
2.
Client *Personal Library Software*
Designers Amanda Grupe, Michael B. Raso
3.
Client *National Telephone Cooperative Association*
Designers John Nettleton, Michael B. Raso
4.
Client *American Association of Spinal Cord Injury Nurses*

5.
Client *Rutgers University School of Management*
6.
Client *American Corporate Counsel Association*
Designers Michael B. Raso, Beth Ready
7.
Client *OPASTCO*
Designers Amanda Grupe, Beth Ready
(opposite)
Client *Fluoroware, Inc.*
Design Firm **Larsen Design + Interactive**
Art Director Richelle Huff
Designer Todd Mannes

1.

2.

3.

4.

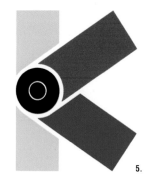

5.

AGRADO™
Feed Ingredient by **Solutia**

6.

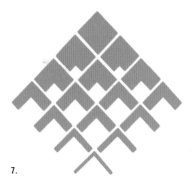

7.

AQUASTAR

8.

9.

10.

11.

12.

MERIDIAN PARTNERS

INCORPORATED   14.

13.

15.

1.

2.

3.

4.

5.

6.

7.

1, 3, 4		**4.**	
Design Firm	**Sacks Design Group**	Client	*Keller Photography*
2, 5, 7		Designer	Jaye H. Sacks
Design Firm	**Gardner Design**	**5.**	
6		Client	*Cat Hospital of Wichita*
Design Firm	**Lumina Studios**	Designer	Bill Gardner
1.		**6.**	
Client	*Overland Trading Co.*	Client	*Overland Trading Co.*
Designers	Jaye H. Sacks, Kathryn Klein	Designers	Jaye H. Sacks, Kathryn Klein
2.		**7.**	
Client	*Cowley County Community College*	Client	*Anastasia Marie Cosmetics*
Designers	Bill Gardner, Brian Miller	Designer	Brian Miller
3.		**(opposite)**	
Client	*Feldman Photography*	Client	*Hilbert Interactive Group*
Designer	Jaye H. Sacks	Design Firm	**Hal Apple Design**
		Designers	Jason Hashmi, Hal Apple

1.

2.

3.

4.

5.

6.

7.

8.

THE CAT

9.

B R A V O ▪ B U S

10.

ARTISAN

11.

12.

13.

RED MOUNTAIN PARK

14.

15. THE MERIT SYSTEM

(all)
Design Firm **DogStar**

1.
Client   *University of Montevallo Falcons*
Designers   Jeff Martin, Rodney Davidson

2.
Client   *Cigar Aficionado Magazine*
Designer   Rodney Davidson

3.
Client   *Billy's*
Designers   Vicki Schenck-Atha,
     Rodney Davidson

4.
Client   *AIGA—*
     (jacket icon for) Ecology of Design
Designers   Brian Collins, Rodney Davidson

5.
Client   *Birmingham Ecoplex*
Designers   Charles Black, Stefanie Becker—
     Gillis Adv.; Rodney Davidson—
     DogStar

6.
Client   *Beaver Construction*
Designers   Terry Slaughter—Slaughter Hanson;
     Rodney Davidson

7.
Client   *Typhoon*
Designers   Barbara Lee—Suka & Friends;
     Rodney Davidson

8.
Client   *DogStar*
Designer   Rodney Davidson

9.
Client   *The Cat/Northumberland*
Designers   Bruce Hamilton—Target Marketing;
     Rodney Davidson

10.
Client   *Birmingham Metropolitan*
     Arts Council
Designer   Rodney Davidson

11.
Client   *Artisan FIlms*
Designers   Laura Marince, Karen Hostetter,
     Rodney Davidson

12.
Client   *Kirk Alford*
Designer   Rodney Davidson

13.
Client   *Supon Design Group/*
     Intnl logos & TM 3
Designer   Rodney Davidson

14.
Client   *Red Mountain Park*
Designers   Gregory Hodges—Hodges &
     Associates; Rodney Davidson

15.
Client   *Ther Merit System/*
     Jefferson Co. Personnel Board
Designers   Gregory Hodges—Hodges &
     Associates; Rodney Davidson—
     DogStar

1.

2.

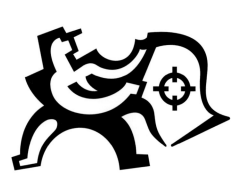

3.

4.

5.

6.

𝒢 L O R Y

7.

1, 4, 5
Design Firm **Pat Jenkins Design**
2, 3, 6, 7
Design Firm **Gardner Design**
1.
  Client   *ATDC*
  Designer   Pat Jenkins
2.
  Client   *Wichita State Uniersity*
           Men's Crew Team
  Designer   Brian Miller
3.
  Client   *International Association of*
           Printing House Craftsmen
  Designers   Brian Miller, Bill Gardner
4.
  Designer   Pat Jenkins

5.
  Client   *Making America Work*
  Designer   Pat Jenkins
6.
  Client   *Wichita State University*
           Shocker Crew Team
  Designer   Brian Miller
7.
  Client   *GLORY*
  Designers   Bill Gardner, Karen Hogn
(opposite)
  Client   *Old Capitol Mall*
  Design Firm **FRCH Design Worldwide**
           (Cincinnati)
  Designers   Michael Beeghly, Erik Brown

OLD CAPITOL
M · A · L · L

47

1.

2.

3.

4.

1ST
NATIONWIDE
BANK
A FEDERAL SAVINGS BANK

5.

6.

7.

LOOSE

Levi's

8.

9.

10.

12.

EurekaBank

11.

14.

13.

KAYAK
S Y S T E M

15.

1, 4, 5, 8, 10, 11, 14, 15
Design Firm **SBG Enterprise**
2, 3, 6, 7, 9, 12, 13
Design Firm **Gardner Design**
1.
Client   *Cheskin+Masten/ImageNet*
Designer   Jessie McAnulty
2.
Client   *Gardner Design*
Designer   Bill Gardner
3.
Client   *Auto Craft*
Designer   Bill Gardner
4.
Client   *California State Lottery*
Designer   Mark Bergman
5.
Client   *1st National Bank*
Designers   Nicolas Sidjakov, Lester Ng
6.
Client   *RVP (Recreational Vehicle Products)*
Designer   Bill Gardner
7.
Client   *Kansas Health Foundation/*
                   Leadership Seminar
Designer   Bill Gardner

8.
Client   *FCB/Honig*
Designer   Paul Woods
9.
Client   *Business Bank of America*
Designer   Bill Gardner
10.
Client   *Berkly System*
Designer   Courtney Reeser
11.
Client   *Eureka Bank*
Designer   Amy Knapp
12.
Client   *Oris Technologies*
Designer   Bill Gardner
13.
Client   *The Independent School*
Designer   Bill Gardner
14.
Designer   Jim Nevins
15.
Client   *Hewlett Packard*
Designer   Thomas Bond

1.

CONNECT

A NORSTAN COMPANY

2.

3.

4.

INFORMATION ADVANTAGE®

5.

7.

6.

1 - 5
Design Firm **Larsen Design + Interactive**
6, 7
Design Firm **Hershey Associates**
8
Design Firm **Jack Nadel, Inc.**

1.
Client   *Opus Corporation*
Creative Director
                Tim Larsen
Art Director   Gayle Jorgens
Designer   Todd Mannes

2.
Client   *Connect Computer*
Art Director   Tim Larsen
Designer   Marc Kundmann

3.
Client   *Imation Corporation*
Creative Director
                Nancy Whittlese
Designers   Sascha Boecker, Todd Nesser

4.
Client   *DEAF*
Creative Director
                Richelle Huff
Designer   Kevin Ylitalo

5.
Client   *Information Advantage*
Creative Director
                Richelle Huff
Designer   Sascha Boecker

6.
Client   *Hamilton Court*
Designers   R. Christine Hershey, Lisa Joss

7.
Client   *Keith-Beer Medical Group*
Designer   R. Christine Hershey

8.
Client   *LifeScan*
Designer   Miguel Rosa
(opposite)
Client   *HOC Industries*
Design Firm   **Gardner Design**
Designer   Brian Miller

8.

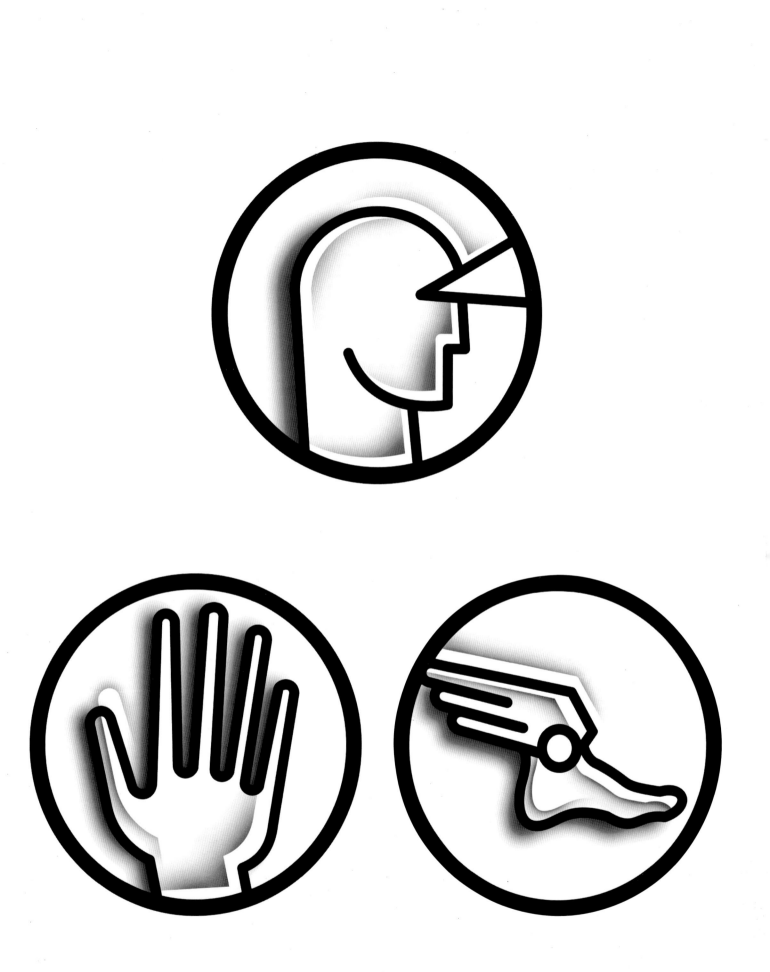

1.

2.

3.

4.

SAN FRANCISCO
SYMPHONY

5.

GIANTS

6.

7.

8.

9.

10.

11.

12.

13.

14.

1, 4, 5, 8, 10, 11, 14, 15
Design Firm **Gardner Design**
2, 3, 6, 7, 9, 12, 13
Design Firm **SBG Enterprise**

1.
Client   *Fat Chance*
Designer Bill Gardner

2.
Client   *3M*
Designer Mary Brucken

4.
Client   *CHiPS*
Designer Bill Gardner

5.
Client   *DeCotiis Erhard Strategic Consulting Group*
Designer Bill Gardner

6.
Client   *SF Symphony*
Designer Paul Wood

7.
Client   *SF Giants*
Designer Kate Greene

8.
Client   *Grider and Company P.A.*
Designer Bill Gardner

9.
Client   *Samaritan*
Designer Jackie Foshaug

10.
Client   *Cramer Calligraphy*
Designer Brian Miller

11.
Client   *Catholic Diocese of Wichita*
Designer Bill Gardner

12.
Client   *Transamerica*
Designer Thomas Bond

13.
Client   *US Air*
Designer Jackie Foshaug

14.
Client   *TumbleDrum*
Designer Bill Gardner

15.
Client   *The Independent School— 3 Level Private School*
Designer Bill Gardner

1.

2.

3.

PRESIDIO
SYSTEMS 4.

Wave**path**

5.

6.

7.

1 - 7
Design Firm **Beggs Design**
Designer   Lee Beggs
1.
   Client   *Vantive*
2.
   Client   *Southern Florida Bank/*
                Wilson Communications
3.
   Client   *University Chiropractic Clinic*
4.
   Client   *Presidio Systems*
5.
   Client   *WavePath/Information Arts Inc.*
6.
   Client   *Cromenco, Inc.*
7.
   Client   *Diane Strongwater*

(opposite)
   Client   *Borders (Cafe Espresso)*
   Design Firm **FRCH Design Worldwide**
                (Cincinnati)
   Designer   Tim Frame

1.

2.

3.

4.

5.

6.

Netfinity

7.

8.

9.

10.

11.

FRONTLINE

12.

```
S R T E C E   F T F S U
N O R T O N   T F S U F
( S E C R E T   S T U F F )
E R S C E T   F U F T S
T E R E C S   U F T S F
```

13.

14.

15.

1, 4, 5, 8, 10, 11, 14, 15
Design Firm **Gardner Design**
2, 3, 6, 7, 9, 12, 13
Design Firm **Gee + Chung Design**
7
Design Firm **Desgrippes Gobé & Associates**
1.
   Client   *Tallgrass Prairie Producers*
   Designers Bill Gardner, Brian Miller
2.
   Client   *Sun Microsystems*
   Art Director, Designer
          Earl Gee
3.
   Client   *Virtual Vineyards*
   Art Directors, Designers
          Earl Gee, Fani Chung
4.
   Client   *Andrews Paint*
   Designer Bill Gardner
5.
   Client   *The Coffee Millers*
   Designer Brian Miller
6.
   Client   *Berman Marketing Reserve*
   Art Director Earl Gee
   Designers Earl Gee, Fani Chung

7.
   Client   *The IBM PC Company*
   Design Director
          Lori Yi
   Sr. Designer Tom Davidson
8.
   Client   *Lazy G Ranch*
   Designers Bill Gardner, Brian Miller
9.
   Client   *Nanocosm Technologies, Inc.*
   Art Directors Earl Gee, Fani Chung
   Designer Fani Chung
10.
   Client   *Community State Bank*
   Designer Bill Gardner
11.
   Client   *Kansas Humane Society*
   Designer Bill Gardner
12.
   Client   *Frontline Now!*
   Art Director Earl Gee
   Designers Earl Gee, Fani Chung
13.
   Client   *Symantec Corporation*
   Art Director, Designer
          Earl Gee
14.
   Client   *Button Heaven*
   Designer Bill Gardner
15.
   Client   *Kansas State University*
   Designer Brian Miller

NysAir
2.

McLean County Prenatal Clinic
1.

3.

TRANSFORMING
OUR ENERGY   4.

C C A N

P R I S M
S Y S T E M
5.

6.

7.

1
    Design Firm **John Walker Graphic Design**
2 - 6
    Design Firm **Michael Orr + Associates, Inc.**
7
    Design Firm **J. Robert Faulkner**
1.
    Client   *McLean County Prenatal Clinic*
    Designer   John Walker
2.
    Client   *NYSAIR/NYSEG*
    Designer   Michael R. Orr
3.
    Client   *Corning Incorporated*
    Designer   Michael R. Orr

4.
    Client   *NYSEG*
    Designers   Michael R. Orr, Gregory Duell
5.
    Client   *The Gunlocke Company*
    Designers   Michael R. Orr, Gregory Duell
6.
    Client   *CCAN*
    Designers   Michael R. Orr, Gregory Duell
7.
    Client   *World Education Center*
    Designer   J. Robert Faulkner
(opposite)
    Client   *Post Tools*
    Design Firm **SBG Enterprise**
    Designer   Thomas Bond

1.

2.

3.

Array

4.

5.

L A M O P

L A M O P

6.

7.

Quester
Technology

8.

60

d / M

9.

AVEO

10.

INVENTA

11.

BOLT

12.

PROTIX

13.

14.

15.

1, 4, 5, 8, 10, 11, 14, 15
Design Firm **Beggs Design**
2, 3, 6, 7, 9, 12, 13
Design Firm **Planet Design Company**

1.
| Client | Logitech, Inc. |
| Designer | Lee Beggs |

2.
| Client | Mirror Mountain Motorcycles |
| Designers | Kevin Wade, Tom Jenkins |

3.
| Client | Misty River Woodworks |
| Designer | Martha Graettinger |

4.
| Client | Array Technology |
| Designer | Lee Beggs |

5.
| Client | Lightgate, Inc. |
| Designer | Lee Beggs |

6.
| Client | La Mop Hair Studio |
| Designer | Kevin Wade |

7.
| Client | Kaz Technologies |
| Designers | Kevin Wade, Martha Graettinger |

8.
| Client | Quester Technology/ AL Shultz Advertising |
| Designer | Lee Beggs |

9.
| Client | Design Milwaukee |
| Designer | Kevin Wade |

10.
| Client | AVEO, Inc. |
| Designer | Lee Beggs |

11.
| Client | Inventa Inc. |
| Designer | Lee Beggs |

12.
| Client | Sherpa |
| Designers | Darci Bechen, Kevin Wade |

13.
| Client | ProTix, Inc. |
| Designers | Ben Hirby, Dana Lytle |

14.
| Client | Saratoga Semiconductor |
| Designer | Lee Beggs |

15.
| Client | Matra Systems/ Wilson Communications |
| Designer | Lee Beggs |

1.

2.

3.

4.

5.

B E R B E E

6.

7.

1 - 3, 6
Design Firm **Planet Design Company**
4, 5
Design Firm **CWA, Inc.**
7
Design Firm **Heather Brook Graef**

1.
Client   *Adams Outdoor Advertising*
Designers   Martha Graettinger, Kevin Wade

2.
Client   *Natural Nylon*
Designer   Kevin Wade

3.
Client   *Salisbury Studios*
Designers   Raelene Mercer, Kevin Wade

4.
Client   *Navatek Ships*
Designers   Susan Merritt, Calvin Woo

5.
Client   *Pasternak*
Designers   Susan Merritt, Calvin Woo

6.
Client   *Berbee Information Networks Corp.*
Designers   James Karlin, Kevin Wade

7.
Client   *John Wilmer Studioworkshop*
             Antique Restoration & Upholstery
Designer   Heather Brook Graef

(opposite)
Client   *Embassy Suites*
Design Firm **SBG Enterprise**
Designer   Paul Woods

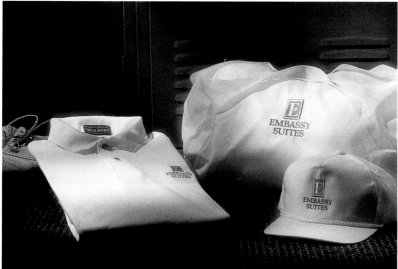

1.

2.

3.

4.

5.

6.

7.

8.

64

9.

10.

11.

12.

TE|A|N|OPHY

13.

14.

15.

(all)		
Design Firm	**David Lemley Design**	
Designer	David Lemley	
1.		
Client	*Starbucks Coffee—Lyre*	
2.		
Client	*Starbucks Coffee—Ethiopia Yergacheffe*	
3.		
Client	*Starbucks Coffee*	
4.		
Client	*Starbucks Coffee—Ship According to Timothy Leary*	
5.		
Client	*Starbucks Coffee—La Sirena*	
6.		
Client	*Starbucks Coffee—Kenya Decaf*	

7.	
Client	*Starbucks Coffee—Kenya*
8.	
Client	*Starbucks Coffee—Yukon Blend*
9.	
Client	*O'Brien International*
10.	
Client	*B-WILD*
11.	
Client	*Dark Horse Clothing*
12.	
Client	*Microsoft*
13.	
Client	*Active Voice*
14.	
Client	*Muzak*
15.	
Client	*Microsoft*

DISTINCTIVE GLOBAL SEAFOOD

1.

It's Time To Eat!

2.

3.

Asian Inspired Contemporary Cuisine

4.

5.

6.

7.

8.

10.

9.

11.

12.

13.

14.

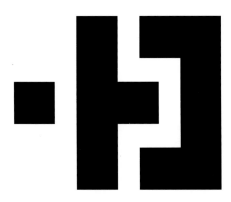

15.

1 -6, 9
Design Firm **Adkins/Balchunas**
7
Design Firm **Sibley/Peteet Design**
8, 10
Design Firm **CWA, Inc.**
11, 12
Design Firm **Gauger & Silva**
13-14
Design Firm **Kollberg/Johnson Associates**
15
Design Firm **Olver Dunlop Associates**

1.
Client   *107 Ocean Bistro*
Designers   Jerry Balchunas, Matt Fernberger

2.
Client   *Eli's Roadhouse*
Designer   Jerry Balchunas

3.
Client   *Hyland Printing*
Designers   Jerry Balchunas, Dan Stebbings

4.
Client   *Lemongrass*
Designers   Jerry Balchunas, Matt Fernberger

5.
Client   *Tortilla Ventures*
Designers   Jerry Balchunas, Dan Stebbings

6.
Client   *Cafe Paragon*
Designers   Jerry Balchunas, Micheline Bouju,
  Michelle Phaneuf

7.
Client   *ChoiceCom*
Designer   Mark Brinkman

8.
Client   *Crest International*
Designers   Susan Merritt, Calvin Woo

9.
Client   *The Art Studio*
Designer   Jerry Balchunas

10.
Client   *Solectek*
Designers   Calvin Woo, Christy Vandeman,
  Leah Hewitt

11.
Client   *Dividend*
Designers   David Gauger, Lori Murphy

12.
Client   *Giro*
Designers   Bob Ankers, David Gauger

13.
Client   *Weiler Brush Company*
Designer   Gary Kollberg

14.
Client   *Kollberg/Johnson Associates*
Designer   Michael Carr

15.
Client   *Beecken Petty & Company*
Designer   Courtney O'Shea

1.

2.

POND'S®

3.

4.

5.

6.

7.

cosmetic associates

8.

9.

10.

11.

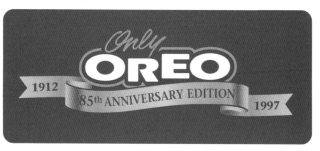

12.

13.

14.

15.

(all)
Design Firm **Hans Flink Design Inc.**

1.
Client   *Colgate Palmolive*
Designers   Mark Krukowis, Susan Kunschaft, Chang Mei Lin, Mike Troian

2.
Client   *Procter & Gamble*
Designers   Hans D. Flink, Stephen Hooper

3.
Client   *Chesebrough-Pond's*
Designers   Hans D. Flink, Chang Mei Lin, Mark Krukowis

4.
Client   *Alberto Culver*
Designers   Hans D. Flink, Mark Krukowis, Chang Mei Lin

5.
Client   *Chesebrough-Pond's*
Designers   Susan Kunschaft, Mark Krukowis

6.
Client   *Alberto Culver*
Designers   Mark Krukowis

7.
Client   *Nestlé*
Designers   Hans D. Flink, Stephen Hooper, Chang Mei Lin

8.
Client   *Cosmetic Associates*
Designer   Hans D. Flink

9.
Client   *Bayer Corp.*
Designers   Hans D. Flink, Stephen Hooper, Suzanne Clark

10.
Client   *Fabergé*
Designers   Hans D. Flink, Chang Mei Lin, Stephen Hooper

11.
Client   *Hofbauer Vienna Ltd.*
Designers   Hans D. Flink, Jane Parasczak

12.
Client   *Nabisco*
Designers   Susan Kunschaft, Mike Troian

13.
Client   *Unilever HPC, USA*
Designers   Mark Krukowis, Susan Kunschaft, Mike Troian, Chang Mei Lin

14.
Client   *SCIMAT Scientific Machinery, Inc.*
Designer   Hans D. Flink

15.
Client   *Procter & Gamble*
Designers   Hans D. Flink, Chris Dane, Stephen Hooper

Telecel

1.

Norelco

2.

3.

geek

4 3 3 5

4.

Mentadent®

5.

Merrill Lynch

6.

shades

7.

Ameritrust

8.

United States Post Office

9.

10.

Z O ë

Pan-Asian Caf
and catering company

11.

Z O ë

Pan-Asian Caf
and catering company

12.

KING·CASEY

BRAND·RETAIL INNOVATORS

13.

CHRYSALIS

14.

15.

1, 2, 6, 8, 9, 10, 13
  Design Firm **King Casey Inc.**
3, 7, 15
  Design Firm **Lotas Minard Patton McIver**
11, 12
  Design Firm **The Puckett Group**
4
  Design Firm **Fairly Painless Advertising**
5
  Design Firm **Hans Flink Design Inc.**
14
  Design Firm **Augusta Design Group**

1.
  Client   *Telecel*
  Designer   John Chrzanowski

2.
  Client   *Norelco*
  Designer   King Casey

3.
  Client   *Lotas Minard Patton McIver*
  Designers Lotus Minard Patton McIver

4.
  Client   *Miller SQA*
  Designers Steve Frykholm, Brian Hauch

5.
  Client   *Unilever HPC, USA*
  Designers Hans D. Flink, Chang Mei Lin, Harry Bentschmann

6.
  Client   *Merrill Lynch*
  Designer   King Casey

7.
  Client   *Renaissance Cosmetics Inc.*
  Designer   Lotas Minard Patton McIver

8.
  Client   *Ameritrust*
  Designer   King Casey

9.
  Client   *United States Postal Service*
  Designers Gene Casey, John Chrzanowski

10.
  Client   *United States Postal Service*
  Designers John Chrzanowski, Steve Brent

11.
  Client   *Zoë Pan-Asian Café*
  Designer   Candy Freund

12.
  Client   *Zoë Pan-Asian Café*
  Designer   Candy Freund

13.
  Client   *King Casey Inc.*
  Designers John Chrzanowski, Steve Brent

14.
  Client   *Chrysalis*
  Designer   Megan Ploska

15.
  Client   *Renaissance Cosmetics Inc.*
  Designer   Lotas Minard Patton McIver

MAKEUP THAT PERFORMS

MAX FACTOR

1.

2.

GENERATOR

DIGITAL POST PRODUCTION

3.

JADE

4.

5.

6.

7.

8.

9.

10.

11.

S A B A N

12.

DIRECTV

13.

ELIZABETH A GIBB ARCHITECT
243 CONCORD AVENUE #3 CAMBRIDGE, MA 02138

14.

IMPROVED
PACKAGING

15.

AFTER HOURS
DESIGN▸ADVERTISING

1.

2.

3.

ASPEN
HOME SYSTEMS

5.

6.

7.

1	Design Firm	**After Hours Design & Advertising**	**4.**	Client	*Phillips Design*

1
Design Firm **After Hours Design & Advertising**
2, 3, 6, 7
Design Firm **Imtech Communications**
4
Design Firm **Phillips Design**
5
Design Firm **Arthur Andersen, LLP**

1.
Client   *After Hours Design & Advertising*
Designer Elizabeth Shott
2.
Client   *Treasures of China*
Designer Robert Keng
3.
Client   *Aspen Home Systems*
Designer Robert Keng

4.
Client   *Phillips Design*
Designer Michael V. Phillips
5.
Client   *Andersen Consulting*
Designer Ilia M. Wood
6.
Client   *Data Architects*
Designer Robert Keng
7.
Client   *Transworld Lubricants, Inc.*
Designer Robert Keng
(opposite)
Client   *TNT*
Design Firm **Pittard Sullivan**

1.

Corrin

3.

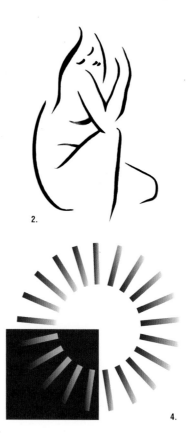

4.

5.

ORIGINALIS

6.

Machado & Associates

A D V E R T I S I N G

7.

B B - I N T E R A C T I V E

8.

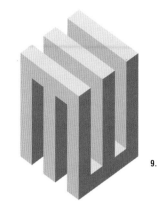

9.

10.

11.

Maitri

12.

FLEA · FOR · ALL
FLEA MARKET OF BRIGHT IDEAS

13.

ColorAd Printers 14.

15.

1, 5, 10, 11, 15
   Design Firm **Michael Doret Graphic Design**
3, 7, 9, 14
   Design Firm **Takigawa Design**
4, 12
   Design Firm **Becca Smidt**
6, 8
   Design Firm **Cawrse + Effect**
2
   Design Firm **Studio Archetype**
13
   Design Firm **Hallmark Cards**
1.
   Client *Fuddruckers*
   Designer Michael Doret
2.
   Client *Avenue Skin Care*
   Designer Andrew Cawrse
3.
   Client *Corrin Produce*
   Designer Jerry Takigawa
4.
   Client *Palo Alto Utilities*
   Designer Becca Smidt
5.
   Client *NBA Properties*
   Designer Michael Doret

6.
   Client *Originalis*
   Designer Andrew Cawrse
7.
   Client *Machado & Associates*
   Designers Jerry Takigawa, Jay Galster
8.
   Client *BB - Interactive*
   Designer Andrew Cawrse
9.
   Client *Mark Watson Building & Renovation*
   Designer Glenn Johnson
10.
   Client *Chic-A-Boom*
   Designer Michael Doret
11.
   Client *Graphic Artists Guild*
   Designer Michael Doret
12.
   Client *Maitri Aids Hospice*
   Designer Becca Smidt
13.
   Client *Flea•For•All Idea Group*
   Designers James Caputo, Jim Ramirez
14.
   Client *ColorAd Printers*
   Designers Jay Galster, Jerry Takigawa
15.
   Client *Coolsville Records*
   Designer Michael Doret

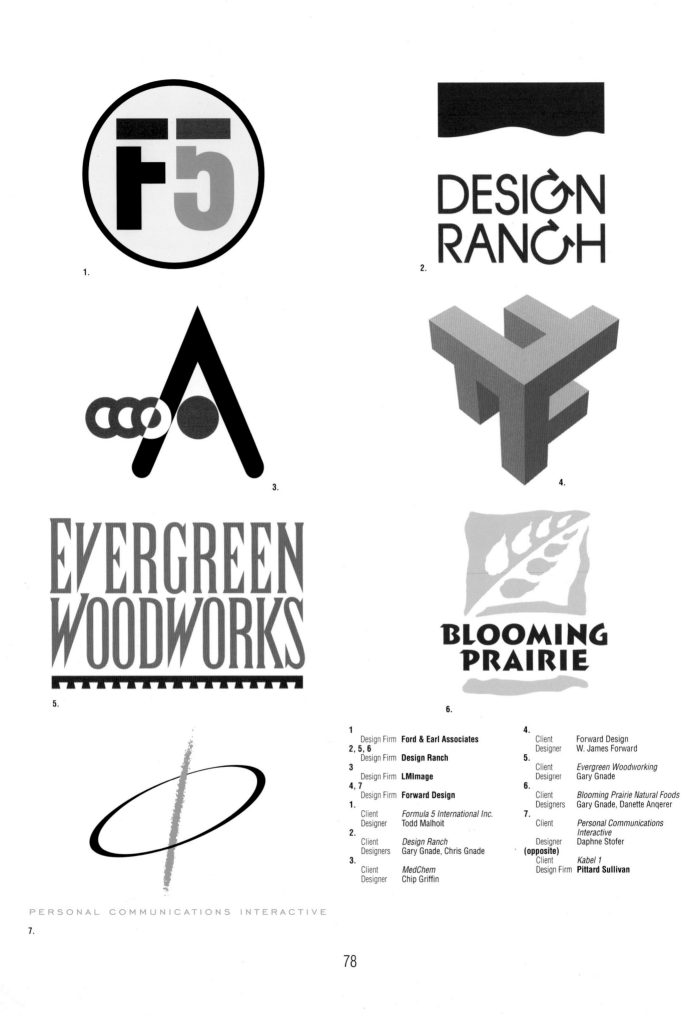

1.

2.

3.

4.

5.

6.

1
Design Firm **Ford & Earl Associates**
2, 5, 6
Design Firm **Design Ranch**
3
Design Firm **LMImage**
4, 7
Design Firm **Forward Design**

1.
Client   *Formula 5 International Inc.*
Designer   Todd Malhoit
2.
Client   *Design Ranch*
Designers   Gary Gnade, Chris Gnade
3.
Client   *MedChem*
Designer   Chip Griffin

4.
Client   *Forward Design*
Designer   W. James Forward
5.
Client   *Evergreen Woodworking*
Designer   Gary Gnade
6.
Client   *Blooming Prairie Natural Foods*
Designers   Gary Gnade, Danette Angerer
7.
Client   *Personal Communications Interactive*
Designer   Daphne Stofer
(opposite)
Client   *Kabel 1*
Design Firm   **Pittard Sullivan**

PERSONAL COMMUNICATIONS INTERACTIVE

7.

KABEL 1

1.

earthsource℠

POWER FOR A NEW WORLD

2.

3.

NATIONAL POLICY AND
RESOURCE CENTER ON
WOMEN & AGING

4.

ENVIROSEP

5.

6.

SMARTSHIELD®

7.

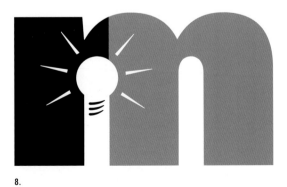

8.

80

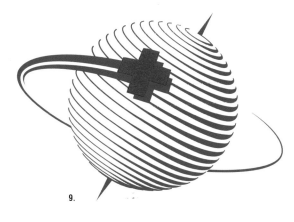

9.

10.

WESTERN

11.

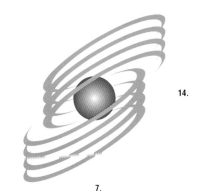

12.

14.

13.

15. **avstar**

1, 2, 9, 15
   Design Firm **Perceive, LLC**
3, 8, 11, 12
   Design Firm **Blevins Design**
6,7,10,13,14
   Design Firm **Dean Corbitt Studio**
4
   Design Firm **Susan Bercu Design Studio**
5
   Design Firm **Sorrell Co.**

1.
   Client   *Aerotech*
   Designer   John White
2.
   Client   *Edison Source*
   Designers   Dave Matea, Scott Littlejohn
3.
   Client   *Security Associates International*
   Designers   Brian Blevins, Chris Blevins
4.
   Client   *National Policy & Resource Center
                on Women & Aging*
   Designer   Susan Bercu
5.
   Client   *Envirosep*
   Designer   Angela Berlingeri
6.
   Client   *Ovarian Cancer Detection &
                Prevention Center (Hawaii)*
   Designer   Dean Corbitt

7.
   Client   *SmartShield Sunscreens, LTD.*
   Designer   Dean Corbitt
8.
   Client   *Robinson Marketing*
   Designer   Brian Blevins
9.
   Client   *National Physicians Network*
   Designer   John White
10.
   Client   *Phoenix Ventures*
   Designer   Dean Corbitt
11.
   Client   *Western Humidor*
   Designers   Brian Blevins, Chris Blevins
12.
   Client   *Anderson Shumaker*
   Designer   Brian Blevins
13.
   Client   *Title Nine Sports*
   Designer   Dean Corbitt
14.
   Client   *Communication Concepts, Inc./
                Service Strategies International, Inc.*
   Designer   Dean Corbitt
15.
   Client   *IVS*
   Designers   Jamie Graupner, Dave Matea, Scott
                Littlejohn, Nora Singer

bailey design group inc.

1.

GOLDEN GLOVES

2.

3.

T*RANS*C*ORE*

4.

Fresh Mark

5.

Environmental Accounting Project

6.

7.

1, 4, 5
Design Firm **Bailey Design Group, Inc.**
2, 6
Design Firm **Levine and Associates**
3, 7
Design Firm **1-earth GRAPHICS**
1.
  Client   *Bailey Design Group, Inc.*
  Art Directors Ken Cahill, David Fiedler
  Designer   Gary LaCroix
2.
  Client   *United Brotherhood of Carpenters*
  Designer   Lena Markley
3.
  Client   *Miami County Recovery Council*
  Designer   Lisa Harris
4.
  Client   Transcore
  Art Director David Fiedler
  Designer   Laura Markley

5.
  Client   *Fresh Mark Inc.*
  Designer   Bailey Design Group, Inc.
6.
  Client   *Environmental Protection Agency*
  Designer   Andrew Criss
7.
  Client   *Cornerstone Natural Foods*
  Designer   Lisa Harris
  (opposite)
  Client   *DNA Plant Technologies*
  Design Firm **Bailey Design Group, Inc.**
  Art Director David Fiedler
  Designer   Stephen R. Perry

Try FreshWorld Farms Tomatoes. Enjoy the differenc

PLAYERS INC ™

1.

2.

3.

CLERMONT
Nursing & Convalescent Center

4.

PARADIGM ™
COMMUNICATION GROUP

5.

SMITHSONIAN
STUDY TOURS

6.

7.

IMPACT
ENGINEERING SOLUTIONS, INC.

8.

9.

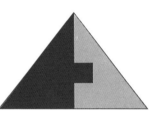

IAMS
COMPANY

10.

CINCRON
AUTOMATED PALLET CELL

11.

ALEXANDER
CONSTRUCTION INC.

12.

WESTLAKE
SURGICAL
C E N T E R

13.

NEW YORK UNIVERSITY
School of Continuing and
Professional Studies

14.

MLSPA™

15.

1, 3, 6, 15
Design Firm **Grafik Communications, Ltd.**
2, 8
Design Firm **The Rittenhouse Group**
4, 5, 10, 11
Design Firm **Pavone Fite Fulwiler**
7
Design Firm **UniWorld Group, Inc.**
9
Design Firm **Yvonne Fitzner Design**
12
Design Firm **LaFond Design**
13
Design Firm **Belyea Design Alliance**
14
Design Firm **O & J Design, Inc.**

1.
Client *Player's Inc.*
Designers David Collins, Judy Kirpich
2.
Client *CAFFE A go go*
Designer Shelby Keefe
3.
Client *American Zoo & Aquarium
Association*
Designers David Collins, Susan English,
Judy Kirpich
4.
Client *Clermont Nursing &
Convalescent Center*
Designer Jeff D. Fulwiler
5.
Client *Paradigm Communication Group*
Designer Jeff D. Fulwiler

6.
Client *Smithsonian Institution*
Designers Lynn Umemoto, Judy Kirpich
7.
Client *Acapulco Black Film Festival*
Designer Vincent St. Vincent
8.
Client *Impact Engineering Solutions, Inc.*
Designer Jason Evans
9.
Client *La Cabana*
Designer Yvonne Fitzner
10.
Client *The Iams Company*
Designer Jeff D. Fulwiler
11.
Client *Cincinnati Milacron*
Designer Jeff D. Fulwiler
12.
Client *J. L. Alexander Group*
Designer Lori LaFond LaMore
13.
Client *Westlake Surgical Center*
Designer Samantha Hunt
14.
Client *New York University School of
Continuing and Professional Studies*
Designers Andrzej J. Olejniczak,
Leslie M. Nayman, Christina Mueller
15.
Client *Major League Soccer
Players Association*
Designers David Collins, Judy Kirpich

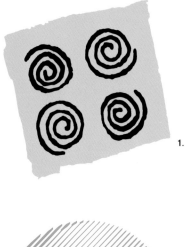

1.

2.

3.

4.

5.

6.

M A R K E T
S C I E N C E S

7.

FONTAINE'S

8.

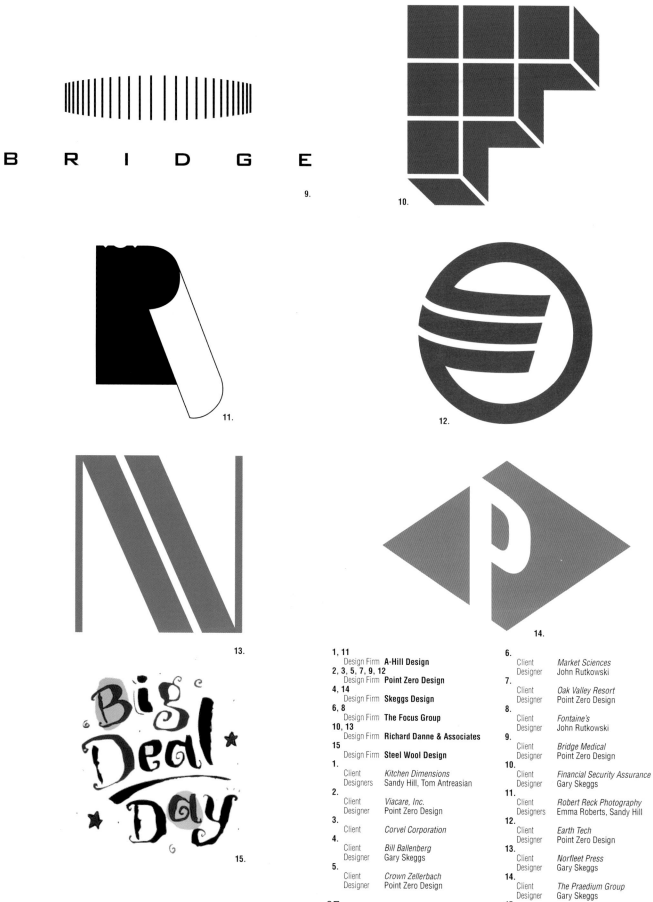

BRIDGE

9.

10.

11.

12.

13.

14.

15.

1, 11
Design Firm **A-Hill Design**
2, 3, 5, 7, 9, 12
Design Firm **Point Zero Design**
4, 14
Design Firm **Skeggs Design**
6, 8
Design Firm **The Focus Group**
10, 13
Design Firm **Richard Danne & Associates**
15
Design Firm **Steel Wool Design**

1.
Client *Kitchen Dimensions*
Designers Sandy Hill, Tom Antreasian
2.
Client *Viacare, Inc.*
Designer Point Zero Design
3.
Client *Corvel Corporation*
4.
Client *Bill Ballenberg*
Designer Gary Skeggs
5.
Client *Crown Zellerbach*
Designer Point Zero Design

6.
Client *Market Sciences*
Designer John Rutkowski
7.
Client *Oak Valley Resort*
Designer Point Zero Design
8.
Client *Fontaine's*
Designer John Rutkowski
9.
Client *Bridge Medical*
Designer Point Zero Design
10.
Client *Financial Security Assurance*
Designer Gary Skeggs
11.
Client *Robert Reck Photography*
Designers Emma Roberts, Sandy Hill
12.
Client *Earth Tech*
Designer Point Zero Design
13.
Client *Norfleet Press*
Designer Gary Skeggs
14.
Client *The Praedium Group*
Designer Gary Skeggs
15.
Client *Hallmark Cards, Inc.*
Designer Kristy D. Lewis

87

1.

Species Survival Plan

2.

3.

4.

5.

6.

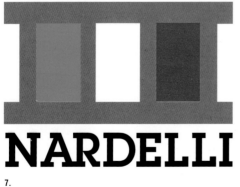

7.

1
Design Firm **IE Design**
2, 5
Design Firm **Brookfield Zoo Design Department**
3, 4, 6, 7
Design Firm **Fleury Design**
1.
Client *American Isuzu Motors Inc.*
Designer Marcie Carson
2.
Client *American Zoo and Aquarium Association*
Designer Hannah Jennings
3.
Client *Fleury Design*
Designer Ellen Fleury
4.
Client *Accurate Typing Service, Inc.*
Designer Ellen Fleury

5.
Client *Brookfield Zoo*
Designer Hannah Jennings
Illustrator Edie Emmenegger
6.
Client *Bagel Heaven*
Designer Ellen Fleury
7.
Client *Nardelli Associates*
Designer Ellen Fleury
(opposite)
Client *Brookfield Zoo*
Design Firm **Brookfield Zoo Design Department**
Designer Hannah Jennings
Illustrator Steve Stratakos

1.

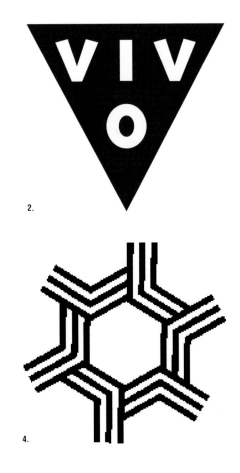

2.

Franchini

3.

4.

S C H O O N O V E R

5.

6.

7.

8.

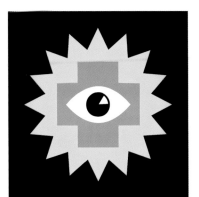

9.

10.

11.

12.

13.

14.

15.

DRAKE DUNN

1.

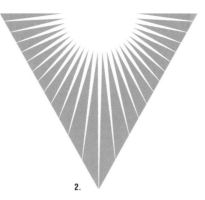

2.

WEST LINN PAPER COMPANY

3.

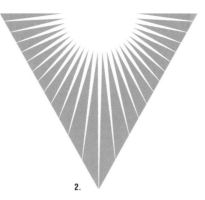

4.

I C T V

5.

NETWORK
POWER & LIGHT

6.

GR95W

7.

VIANT

8.

9.

10.

INKTOMI
CORPORATION

11.

WILLOWS
SOFTWARE

12.

13.

14.

15.

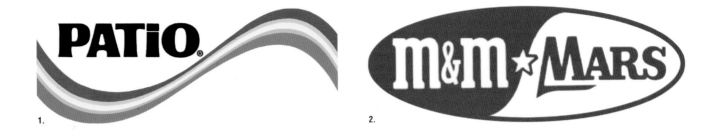

1.

2.

3.

4.

5.

6.

SKILCRAFT

7.

(all)
Design Firm **Dixon & Parcels Associates, Inc.**
1.
Client   *R.J.R. Foods, Inc.*
Designers   Dixon & Parcels Associates
2.
Client   *Mars, Inc.*
Designers   Dixon & Parcels Associates
3.
Client   *La Choy Food Products, Inc.*
Designers   Dixon & Parcels Associates
4.
Client   *Borden Inc.*
Designers   Dixon & Parcels Associates

5.
Client   *Crest International*
Designers   Dixon & Parcels Associates
6.
Client   *Superior Brands, Inc.*
Designers   Dixon & Parcels Associates
7.
Client   *Lighthouse for the Blind*
Designers   Dixon & Parcels Associates
(opposite)
Client   *Quaker State Corporation*
Design Firm **Dixon & Parcels Associates, Inc.**

1.

2.

3.

4.

5.

6.

7.

8.

96

9.

Animated
Resolutions

10.

11.

© PENN STATE MCMLXXXIII

12.

GEORGIA
SOUTHERN
U N I V E R S I T Y   14.

13.

MATSURI ™

15.

1, 10, 15
Design Firm **DesignCentre**
2, 3, 4, 5, 6, 8, 9, 11, 12, 13, 14
Design Firm **Dixon & Parcels Associates, Inc.**
7
Design Firm **Chapman and Partners**

1.
Client   Federated Department Stores, Inc.
Designer   Julie Eubanks
2.
Client   Industrial Valley Bank
Designers Dixon & Parcels Associates
3.
Client   Hill Refrigeration
Designers Dixon & Parcels Associates
4.
Client   Dixon & Parcels Associates, Inc.
Designers Dixon & Parcels Associates
5.
Client   BMJ Financial Services, Corporation
Designers Dixon & Parcels Associates
6.
Client   Lehigh University
Designers Dixon & Parcels Associates
7.
Client   Panache Resources &
           Systems Corp.
Designers David Chapman, Carol Besheer

8.
Client   The Bachman Company
Designers Dixon & Parcels Associates
9.
Client   Partnership Ministries Unlimited
Designers Dixon & Parcels Associates
10.
Client   Animated Rsolutions, L.L.C.
Designer   Lance Langdon
11.
Client   Youngs Drug Products Corp.
Designers Dixon & Parcels Associates
12.
Client   The Athletic Department of
           Pennsylvania State University
Designers Dixon & Parcels Associates
13.
Client   Mars, Inc.
Designers Dixon & Parcels Associates
14.
Client   Georgia Southern University
Designers Dixon & Parcels Associates
15.
Client   LensCrafters
Designer   Julie Eubanks

1.

2.

3.

4.

5.

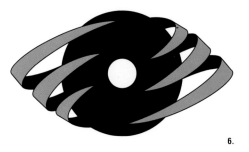

6.

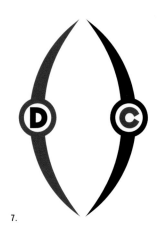

7.

8.

OCEAN SPORTS CLUB

9.

10.

IN TOUCH

11.

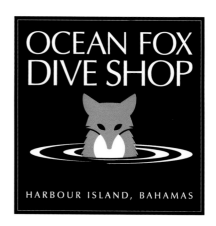

OCEAN FOX DIVE SHOP

HARBOUR ISLAND, BAHAMAS

12.

13.

THE GEGENHEIMER GROUP LTD.

14.

15.

1 - 8
Design Firm **Swieter Design U.S.**
9 - 15
Design Firm **Tom Fowler, Inc.**

1.
Client — *Converse Basketball*
Designers — John Swieter, Kevin Flatt

2.
Client — *Pierce Contracting*
Designer — Mark Ford

3.
Client — *Carman Engineering*
Designers — John Swieter, Mark Ford

4.
Client — *Royal Rack*
Designer — Mark Ford

5.
Client — *Converse Basketball*
Designers — John Swieter, Kevin Flatt

6.
Client — *Ominidia, Inc.*
Designers — John Swieter, Jim Vogel

7.
Client — *Dallas Cowboys Football*
Designers — John Swieter, Mark Ford

8.
Client — *Activerse*
Designers — John Swieter, Mark Ford

9.
Client — *Four Seeds Corporation*
Designer — Thomas G. Fowler

10.
Client — *Ocean Fox Dive Shop*
Designer — Thomas G. Fowler

11.
Client — *NYNEX*
Designer — Karl S. Maruyama

12.
Client — *M-Two*
Designer — Karl S. Maruyama

13.
Client — *Bull's Head Animal Hospital*
Designer — Samuel Toh

14.
Client — *Gegenheimer Group Ltd.*
Designer — Elizabeth P. Ball

15.
Client — *TIAA CREF*
Designers — Elizabeth P. Ball, Thomas G. Fowler

1.

2.

3.

4.

5.

6.

7.

8.

9.

11.

13.

SAN FRANCISCO CLOTHING

975 Lexington Avenue New York, N.Y. 10021 (212) 472-8740

15.

10.

Official Brand

12.

14.

1, 2
   Design Firm **Yuguchi Group, inc.**
3 - 14
   Design Firm **David Lemley Design**
15
   Design Firm **George Tscherny, Inc.**
1.
   Client   *Wells Fargo Bank*
   Designers Clifford Yuguchi, Koji Takei,
           David Brewster
2.
   Client   *SurLuster*
   Designer Clifford Yuguchi
3.
   Client   *E. Alexander Hair Studio*
   Designer David Lemley
4.
   Client   *The Bon Marché via Leslie Phinney*
   Designer David Lemley
5.
   Client   *Overlake Press*
   Designer David Lemley
6.
   Client   *Barry Fishler*
            Direct Response Copywriting

   Designer David Lemley
7.
   Client   *Active Voice*
   Designer David Lemley
8.
   Client   *Nike Boyswear*
   Designer David Lemley
9.
   Client   *David Lemley*
   Designer David Lemley
10.
   Client   *One Reel*
   Designer David Lemley
11.
   Client   *Garden Botanika*
   Designer David Lemley
12.
   Client   *Nike—Official Brand*
   Designer David Lemley
13.
   Client   *Muzak*
   Designer David Lemley
14.
   Client   *Aldus*
   Designer David Lemley
15.
   Client   *San Francisco Clothing*
   Designer George Tscherny

1.

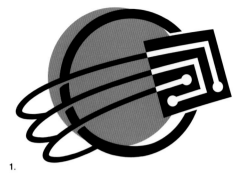

LensBuff ™

2.

DIGITAL
IMAGING
TECHNOLOGY
CENTER

3.

A

ALTEON
NETWORKS

4.

JUNEBUG
F I L M S

5.

R E S O N A T E

6.

7.

1, 2
Design Firm **icon Graphics, Inc.**
3 - 7
Design Firm **Scott Brown Design**
1.
Client   *Eastman Kodak Company*
2.
Client   *Eye Openers*
3.
Client   *Xerox Corp.*
Designer Scott Brown
4.
Client   *Alteon Networks*
Designer Scott Brown
5.
Client   *Junebug Films*
Designer Scott Brown

6.
Client   *Resonate*
Designer Scott Brown
7.
Client   *Scott Brown Design*
Designer Scott Brown
(opposite)
Client   *AVASTOR*
       (Digital Equipment Corporation)
Design Firm **Larsen Design + Interactive**
Creative Director
       Tim Larsen
Art Director Gayle Jorgens
Designers Larsen Design Staff

AVASTOR

TIAN TAN CARPETS
BEIJING

1.

ADENAK

2.

**AFS INTERCULTURAL
PROGRAMS**

3.

E. LEON JIMENES, C. POR A.

4.

UB

UNITED BRANDS

5.

DAINANA
SECURITIES

6.

PUERTO RICO

7.

GANNETT

8.

104

IFT

9.

ZOËTICS

10.

Merrill Lynch Realty

11.

MERCURY

12.

Drackett

13.

CHICOPEE

14.

BANCO DE PONCE

15.

(all)
Design Firm **Yasumura Assoc./
             Muts & Joy & Design**
Designers   Muts
1.
  Client   *Tian-Tan Carpets*
  Designers Muts
2.
  Client   *Adenak*
  Designers Muts
3.
  Client   *AFS*
  Designer   Joy Greene
4.
  Client   *E. Leon Jimenes, C. Por A.*
  Designers Hitomi, Muts
5.
  Client   *United Brands Inc.*
  Designers Muts
6.
  Client   *Dainana Security*
  Designers Muts

7.
  Client   *Puerto Rico Tourism & Commerce*
  Designers Muts
8.
  Client   *Gannett Co.*
  Designers Muts Yasumura
9.
  Client   *IFT*
  Designer   Gisele Sangiovanni
10.
  Client   *Zoetics Inc.*
  Designer   Gisele Sangiovanni
11.
  Client   *Merrill Lynch Realty*
  Designers Muts
12.
  Client   *Mercury*
  Designer   Richard H. Muts
13.
  Client   *Drackett*
  Designer   Andy L. Muts
14.
  Client   *Chicopee*
  Designer   Richard H. Muts
15.
  Client   *Banco De Ponce*
  Designers Muts Yasumura

1.

Knowledge

Action

Performance

2.

3.

4.

5.

6.

7.

1, 2
Design Firm   **McKenzie & Associates**
3 - 7
Design Firm   **aire design company**
1.
Client   *S.M.A.R.T.*
2.
Client   *Ernst & Young—Stanford Project*
3.
Client   *Tucson Electric Power Co.*
Designer   Matthew Rivera
4.
Client   *Arizona International Campus*
Designer   Shari Rykowski

5.
Client   *aire design company*
              (formerly C-Kim Design)
Designer   David Kolb
6.
Client   *Loews Ventana Flying V Bar & Grill*
Designers   Kerry Martyr, Catharine M. Kim
7.
Client   *Avikan International Academies*
Creative Director, Designer, Illustrator
              Catharine M. Kim
Contributors Matthew Rivera, Shari Rykowski
(opposite)
Client   *Minneapolis Planetarium*
Design Firm   **Larsen Design + Interactive**
Creative Director
              Tim Larsen
Designer   Marc Kundmann

MINNEAPOLIS PLANETARIUM

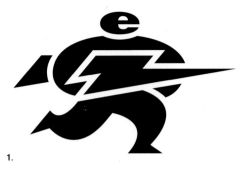

1.

2.

3.

4.

5.

6.

7.

8.

9.

10.

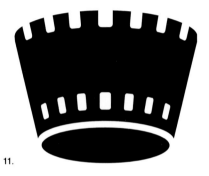

11.

12.

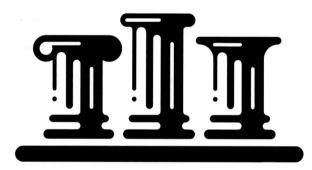

13.

14.

15.

1 - 7, 9 - 13 - 15
Design Firm **Sibley/Peteet Design**
8
Design Firm **The Invisions Group**

1.
Client *EnerShop*
Designer Derek Welch

2.
Client *Vignette*
Designer Mark Brinkman

3.
Client *Boundless Technologies*
Designer Mark Brinkman

4.
Client *Mercury Messenger Service*
Designer Tom Hough

5.
Client *The Container Store*
Designer David Beck

6.
Client *Dal Tile*
Designer Rex Peteet

7.
Client *Halogen Systems*
Designer Mark Brinkman

8.
Client *The Buffalo Club*
Designers Leo Mullen, Michael Kraine

9.
Client *Scotland Yards*
Designer Rex Peteet

10.
Client *Televentures*
Designer Rex Peteet

11.
Client *Mike King Photography*
Designers Rex Peteet, Tom Kirsch

12.
Client *Haggar Apparel Company*
Designer David Beck

13.
Client *American Campus Communities*
Designers Mark Brinkman, Rex Peteet

14.
Client *C-Core*
Designer Brent McMahan

15.
Client *Energy Central*
Designer Mark Brinkman

PUMP
RECORDS

1.

2.

Skirball Cultural Center

3.

MERRITT

4.

M.A. Weatherbie & Co., Inc.

5.

TOSCANA

6.

THE
INVISIONS
GROUP

7.

8.

1, 3, 4, 6
 Design Firm **Kim Baer Design**
2, 5
 Design Firm **Inc 3**
7
 Design Firm **The Invisions Group**
8
 Design Firm **Gams Chicago, Inc.**

1.
 Client   *Pump Records*
 Designer   Liz Roberts
2.
 Client   *Fairhaven Partners*
             Investment Group
 Designers   Harvey Appelbaum,
             Nick Guarracino
3.
 Client   *Skirball Cultural Center*
 Designer   Jennifer Miller
 Illustrator Benjamin Cziller

4.
 Client   *The Merritt Co.*
 Designer   Maxine Mueller
5.
 Client   *Matthew A. Weatherbie & Co., Inc.*
 Designers   Harvey Appelbaum, Nick Guarracino
6.
 Client   *Toscana Restaurant*
 Designer   Barbara Cooper
7.
 Client   *The Invisions Group*
 Designers   Roo Johnson, The Invisions Group
8.
 Client   *Follett Library Resources*
 Designers   John V. Anderson
(opposite)
 Client   *Novellus Systems*
 Design Firm **Larsen Design + Interactive**
 Creative Director
             Tim Larsen
 Art Director Donna Root
 Designer   Sascha Boecker

S P E E D

1.

2.

3.

4.

5.

6.

COMPLETE CONTACT LENS CARE

7.

8.

DARWIN

9.

CDA

Copper Development Association

10.

Com.plete

THE COMPLETE CONNECTION

11.

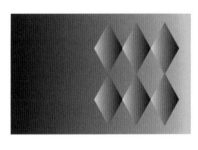

CAPITOL RISK CONCEPTS

12.

C A M B I U M

13.

Argyle Associates

14.

MONTEREY BAY
AQUARIUM

15.

1, 2, 4, 5, 7, 9 - 14
Design Firm **Lee Communications, Inc.**
3, 6, 15
Design Firm **Ace Design**
1.
Client — *Tocqueville Asset Mgmt*
Designers — Bob Lee, Dennis DeFrancesco
2.
Client — *Adgis, Inc.*
Designer — Bob Lee
3.
Client — *Denver Zoo*
Art Director — Richard Graef
Designer — Bonnie Russell
4.
Client — *The Fairchild Corporation*
Designer — Bob Lee
5.
Client — *BAIGlobal Inc.*
Designer — Bob Lee
6.
Designer — Richard Graef
7.
Client — *PuriLens, Inc.*
Designer — Bob Lee

8.
Client — *US Employment Service,*
Dept. of Labor
Designer — Arthur Congdon
9.
Client — *Darwin Asset Management*
Designers — Bob Lee, Dennis DeFrancesco
10.
Client — *Copper Development Assn.*
Designer — Bob Lee
11.
Client — *Com.plete/GlobeWave, Inc.*
Designer — Bob Lee
12.
Client — *Capitol Risk Concepts, Ltd.*
Designers — Bob Lee, Dennis DeFrancesco
13.
Client — *Cambium House, Ltd.*
Designer — Bob Lee
14.
Client — *Argyle Associates, Inc.*
Designer — Bob lee
15.
Client — *Monterey Bay Aquarium*
Designer — Richard Graef

1.

2.

3.

4.

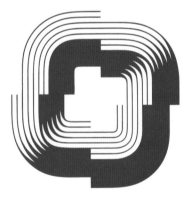

5.

6.

7.

1 - 3, 6			**5.**	
Design Firm	**Lippincott & Margulies, Inc.**		Client	*The Investment Properties Group*
4, 5, 7			Designer	Arthur Congdon
Design Firm	**Congdon Macdonald Inc.**		**6.**	
1.			Client	*The Great Atlantic and*
Client	*Fleetwood Enterprises Inc.*			*Pacific Tea Company*
Designer	Arthur Congdon		Designer	Arthur Congdon
2.			**7.**	
Client	*United Van Lines*		Client	*Hackney (Freeway Oil)*
Designers	Arthur Congdon, Michael Toomey		Designer	Arthur Congdon
3.			**(opposite)**	
Client	*First Union National Bank*		Client	*Coca Cola Co.*
Designer	Arthur Congdon		Design Firm	**SBG Enterprise**
4.			Designers	Vicki Cero, Mary Brucken
Client	*Sports Metaskills*			
Designer	Arthur Congdon			

1.

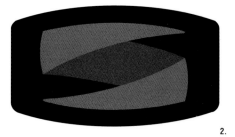

2.

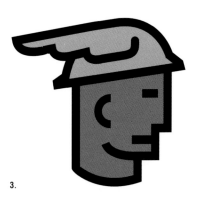

3.

4.

5.

6.

7.

8.

SPARK HOLDINGS

9.

10.

11.

12.

13.

14.

15.

(all)
Design Firm **Swieter Design U.S.**

1.
Client   *Young Presidents' Organization*
Designers   John Swieter, Mark Ford

2.
Client   *Serrano Interiors*
Designers   John Swieter, Mark Ford

3.
Client   *Mercury Messenger*
Designer   Mark Ford

4.
Client   *Sports Lab*
Designer   John Swieter

5.
Client   *Young Presidents' Organization*
Designers   John Swieter, Mark Ford

6.
Client   *Street Savage*
Designers   John Swieter, Mark Ford

7.
Client   *Backdoor Delivery*
Designers   John Swieter, Mark Ford

8.
Client   *Young Presidents' Organization*
Designers   John Swieter, Mark Ford

9.
Client   *Spark Holdings*
Designer   John Swieter

10.
Client   *Uptown Jazz Festival*
Designer   Mark Ford

11.
Client   *T.H. Quest*
Designer   Mark Ford

12.
Client   *Shears*
Designer   Mark Ford

13.
Client   *Shower Head*
Designers   John Swieter, Paul Munsterman

14.
Client   *Vellum Point*
Designer   Mark Ford

15.
Client   *Connectware*
Designer   John Swieter

1.

2.

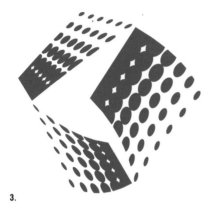

3.

4.

5.

6.

7.

1 - 5
Design Firm **Congdon & Company LLC**
6, 7
Design Firm **Business Graphics Group**
1.
Client   *New Canaan Madrigal Ensemble*
Designer   Arthur Congdon
2.
Client   *New Canaan Madrigal Ensemble*
Designer   Arthur Congdon
3.
Client   *ATMI/Novasource*
Designer   Arthur Congdon
4.
Client   *ATMI/Hypernex*
Designer   Arthur Congdon

5.
Client   *Corpair*
Designer   Arthur Congdon
6.
Client   *Tumi Incorporated*
Art Director   Cam Roberson
Designer   Layne Imada
7.
Client   *Oasys Telecom*
Art Director   Cam Roberson
Designer   Layne Imada
(opposite)
Client   *MetLife*
Design Firm **Yasumura Assoc.,
Muts & Joy & Design**
Designer   Katherine Hames

1.

CAPITOLTOWER

2.

3.

ASSASSINS

L·I·F·E

MANAGER℠

4.

CIRCLE MARKETING

5.

6.

7.

8.

120

9.

FINANCIAL
HORIZONS

10.

11.

Ardco

12.

O R I E N T

A I R L I N E S

A S S O C I A T I O N

13.

14.

Seattle Symphony

15.

1			7.		
	Design Firm	**Gams Chicago, Inc.**		Client	*The Ohio State University*
2 - 10				Designers	Michael Tennyson Smith,
	Design Firm	**Rickabaugh Graphics**			Eric Rickabaugh
11			8.		
	Design Firm	**Rick Eiber Design (RED), RVT Inc.**		Client	*NBA Properties*
12 - 15				Designers	NBA Properties, Tom O'Grady,
	Design Firm	**Rick Eiber Design (RED)**			Eric Rickabaugh
1.			9.		
	Client	*Health & Fitness Center of*		Client	*Run for Christ*
		Oak Brook Hills		Designer	Eric Rickabaugh
	Designer	John V. Anderson	10.		
2.				Client	*Nationwide Insurance*
	Client	*The Galbreath Comany*		Designer	Eric Rickabaugh
	Designer	Eric Rickabaugh	11.		
3.				Client	*UNR Inc.*
	Client	*Players Theatre*		Designer	Rick Eiber
	Designer	Eric Rickabaugh	12.		
4.				Client	*Ardco, Inc.*
	Client	*Nationwide Insurance*		Designer	Rick Eiber, John Fortune
	Designer	Eric Rickabaugh	13.		
5.				Client	*Orient Airlines Assn.*
	Client	*Circle Marketing*		Designer	Rick Eiber
	Designer	Eric Rickabaugh	14.		
6.				Client	*Woodland Investment Co.*
	Client	*Port Columbus Executive Park*		Designer	Rick Eiber
	Designer	Eric Rickabaugh	15.		
				Client	*Seattle Symphony*
				Designer	Rick Eiber

1.

2.

3.

4.

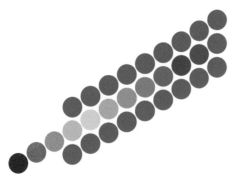

5.

6.

7.

1, 2
Design Firm **Segura Inc**
3, 4
Design Firm **The Majestic Group, Inc.**
5, 6
Design Firm **Allan Miller & Associates**
7
Design Firm **Donaldson, Lufkin & Jenrette**
1.
Client   *Q101 Radio*
Designers   Carlos Segura, Brent Riley
2.
Client   *Sun + Moon*
Designers   Susana Detembleque, Carlos Segura
3.
Client   *Golfdome*
Designer   Stephen E. Nagy

4.
Client   *Jenny Woods Dance*
Designer   Stephen E. Nagy
5.
Client   *Birm*
Designer   Allan Miller
6.
Client   *Acacia Landscape*
Designer   Allan Miller
7.
Client   *Sprout Group*
Designers   DLJ Graphics
(opposite)
Client   *PCEQ*
Design Firm **Yasumura Assoc.,
            Muts & Joy & Design**
Designer   Emi Yasumura

Chicago Pneumatic

1.

Skaneateles Country Club

2.

3.

4.

GERBER

5.

APS

6.

PERFORMANCE MANAGEMENT ASSOCIATES

7.

UNITED STATES POSTAL SERVICE

8.

Medical Transcriptions

9.

MARK
INDUSTRIES
SINCE 1964

10.

PRIME COMPANIES, INC.

11.

RPM
investment

12.

13.

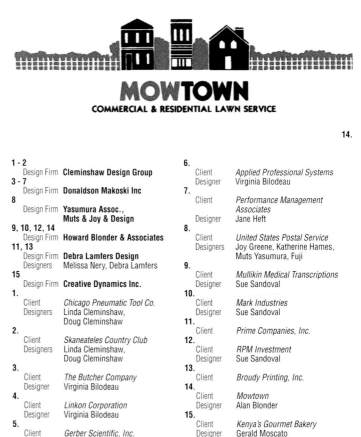

MOWTOWN
COMMERCIAL & RESIDENTIAL LAWN SERVICE

14.

kenya's
GOURMET BAKERY

15.

1 - 2
Design Firm **Cleminshaw Design Group**
3 - 7
Design Firm **Donaldson Makoski Inc**
8
Design Firm **Yasumura Assoc.,**
Muts & Joy & Design
9, 10, 12, 14
Design Firm **Howard Blonder & Associates**
11, 13
Design Firm **Debra Lamfers Design**
Designers Melissa Nery, Debra Lamfers
15
Design Firm **Creative Dynamics Inc.**

1.
Client *Chicago Pneumatic Tool Co.*
Designers Linda Cleminshaw,
Doug Cleminshaw
2.
Client *Skaneateles Country Club*
Designers Linda Cleminshaw,
Doug Cleminshaw
3.
Client *The Butcher Company*
Designer Virginia Bilodeau
4.
Client *Linkon Corporation*
Designer Virginia Bilodeau
5.
Client *Gerber Scientific, Inc.*
Designer Debby Ryan

6.
Client *Applied Professional Systems*
Designer Virginia Bilodeau
7.
Client *Performance Management*
Associates
Designer Jane Heft
8.
Client *United States Postal Service*
Designers Joy Greene, Katherine Hames,
Muts Yasumura, Fuji
9.
Client *Mullikin Medical Transcriptions*
Designer Sue Sandoval
10.
Client *Mark Industries*
Designer Sue Sandoval
11.
Client *Prime Companies, Inc.*
12.
Client *RPM Investment*
Designer Sue Sandoval
13.
Client *Broudy Printing, Inc.*
14.
Client *Mowtown*
Designer Alan Blonder
15.
Client *Kenya's Gourmet Bakery*
Designer Gerald Moscato

1. *Advertising Club* of Greater St. Louis

2.

3.

4.

5.

6. JOURNEYS

7.

8. St. Louis BLUES 25 YEARS ™

9.

Washington's
L A N D I N G

10.

11.

12.

Summit Strategies, Inc.

13.

14.

15.

1, 8, 13
Design Firm **McDermott Design**
2 - 7, 9 - 12, 14, 15
Design Firm **Agnew Moyer Smith**

1.
Client   *Advertising Club of St. Louis*
Designer Bill McDermott

2.
Client   *Pittsburgh Dance Council*
Designer John Sotirakis

3.
Client   *Pittsburgh Zoo*
Designer Reed Agnew

4.
Client   *Pittsburgh Department of
City Planning/ Pittsburgh
Downtown Plan*
Designer John Sotirakis

5.
Client   *Kane Regional Center*
Designer Don Moyer

6.
Client   *Lincoln Elementary School PTA,
Aileen Owens*
Designer Randy Ziegler

7.
Client   *California University of Pennsylvania*
Designer John Sotirakis

8.
Client   *St. Louis Blues, NHL*
Designer Bill McDermott

9.
Client   *Pittsburgh Light Rail Transit System*
Designer Don Moyer

10.
Client   *Washington's Landing*
Designer Jim Curl

11.
Client   *The Benedum Center for the
Performing Arts*
Designer John Sotirakis

12.
Client   *Three Rivers Stadium*
Designer John Sotirakis

13.
Client   *Summit Strategies, Inc.*
Designer Bill McDermott

14.
Client   *Port of Pittsburgh*
Designer Gina Datres

15.
Client   *The San Damiano Players*
Designer John Sotirakis

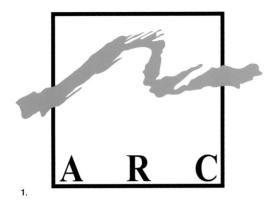

A R C

1.

Rock Creek
TECHNOLOGIES

2.

HOTEL VINTAGE PARK

3.

CK

4.

KIMPTON GROUP™

5.

WORKING

WARRIOR

6.

PastaPomodoro

7.

VISTA CLARA RANCH
resort and spa

8.

130

9.

10.

VISTA

CONTROL SYSTEMS 11.

HOTEL VINTAGE COURT

12.

14.

M I R A G E

13.

THE HOTEL JULIANA

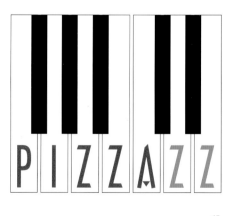

15.

1, 6, 9
Design Firm **The Robin Shepherd Group**
2
Design Firm **Axis Communications**
3, 5, 12, 14
Design Firm **Hunt Weber Clark Associates**
4, 10
Design Firm **E. Christopher Klumb Associates, Inc.**
7, 11, 13, 15
Design Firm **Cisneros Design**
8
Design Firm **Griego Design**

1.
Client *Arc International Inc.*
Designers Tom Schifanella, Robin Shepherd
2.
Client *Rock Creek Technology*
Designers Craig Byers, Chris Paul
3.
Client *Kimpton Hotel Group/ Vintage Park Hotel*
Designers Nancy Hunt-Weber, Gary Williams
4.
Client *E. Christopher Klumb Associates, Inc.*
Designer Christopher Klumb
5.
Client *Kimpton Hotel Group*
Designers Nancy Hunt-Weber, Deborah Dickson

6.
Client *Working Warrior*
Designer Justin Lee
7.
Client *Pasta Pomodoro*
Designer Eric Griego
8.
Client *Vista Clara Ranch*
Designer Eric Griego
9.
Client *Juice n' Java Caffé and Restaurant*
Designer Mike Earnhart
10.
Client *Darien Arts Center*
Designer Christopher Klumb
11.
Client *Vista Control Systems*
Designer Fred Cisneros
12.
Client *Vintage Court Hotel/ Kimpton Hotel Group*
Designers Nancy Hunt-Weber, Christopher Clark
13.
Client *Route 66/Mirage*
Designer Harry Forehand III
14.
Client *The Hotel Juliana/ Kimpton Hotel Group*
Designers Nancy Hunt-Weber, Gary Williams
15.
Client *Pizzaz Sports Bar*
Designer Fred Cisneros

KEHRS MILL
FAMILY DENTAL CARE

1.

The
LEGACY
Group, Inc.

Estate Planning & Asset Protection

2.

BROUGHTON
International

3.

4.

5.

TICKETS
now
MEDIA SERVICES

6.

7.

UNITED STATES
POSTAL SERVICE

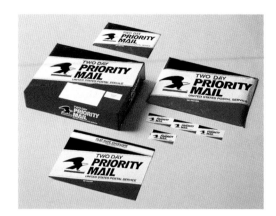

1.

CatheyAssociates,Inc.
Graphic Design & Identity Development

2.

3.

4.

5.

AccuSight

6.

7.

8.

Procurement & Logistics

9.

10.

The Kinsey Institute For Research
in Sex, Gender and Reproduction

11.

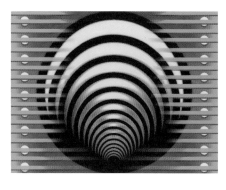

12.

13.

NAqcess℠

14.

Second Opinion
INTERIORS

15.

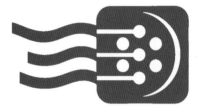

Telcom

1.

I·T·S

2.

FatigueBusters™

3.

omnigraphics

4.

 SONICS

5.

MorseDiesel
Construction/Consulting

6.

MANES   **S P A C E**

7.

8.

PARROT TREE
P L A N T A T I O N

9.

DAVOL

10.

omnigraphics

11.

PADDLEMANIA

12.

13.

Vnet^{sm}

14.

15.

137

1.

2.

MOSS CAIRNS

Raising meetings to new heights

3.

PALE ALE

4.

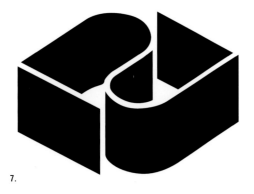

5.

6.

7.

8.

9.

10.

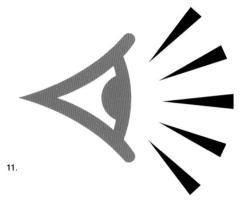

11.

12.

13.

IMAGEMAKER

14.

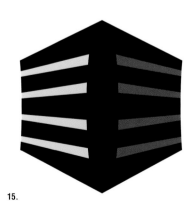

15.

1, 11		
Design Firm	**Oakley Design Studios**	
2		
Design Firm	**Tyler School of Art Graduate Graphic Design Program**	
3		
Design Firm	**Foley Sackett**	
4, 8, 9		
Design Firm	**Lance Anderson Design**	
5, 6, 7, 10, 13, 14, 15		
Design Firm	**Tim Celeski Studios**	
12		
Design Firm	**McGaughy Design**	

1.
Client — *Doug Baldwin • Writer*
Designer — Tim Oakley

2.
Client — *Temple University*
Designer — Kristine F. Herrick

3.
Client — *Moss Cairns*
Designer — Chris Cortilet

4.
Client — *California Cafe*
Designers — Lance Anderson, Richard Escasany

5.
Client — *Kathryn Buffum, DDS*
Designer — Tim Celeski

6.
Client — *Cascade Bike Club*
Designer — Tim Celeski

7.
Client — *Professional Practice Environments*
Designer — Tim Celeski

8.
Client — *S. Asimakopoulas Cafe*
Designer — Lance Anderson

9.
Client — *Michael Bondi Metal Design*
Designer — Lance Anderson

10.
Client — *Interactive Design*
Designer — Tim Celeski

11.
Client — *Meyer Projection Systems*
Designer — Tim Oakley

12.
Client — *Scott Braman Photography*
Designer — Malcolm McGaughy

13.
Client — *Washington Hand Surgery Center*
Designer — Tim Celeski

14.
Client — *Imagemaker Salon*
Designer — Tim Celeski

15.
Client — *Innovation, Inc.*
Designer — Tim Celeski

1.

2.

3.

4.

5.

6.

7.

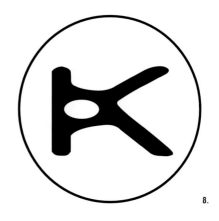

8.

PREMISE

9. COMMUNICATION SYSTEMS

10.

INTEGRATED NETWORK CONCEPTS

11.

12.

KOMAR

13.

a family of sleepwear

DIAMOND EXCHANGE ◆X

14.

VIACOM newmedia ™

15.

1, 2, 3, 7, 10, 12
Design Firm **Selbert Perkins Design Collaborative**

4, 6, 8, 13, 14, 15
Design Firm **Doublespace**

5, 9, 11
Design Firm **Stein & Company**

1.
Client *The Jerde Partnership*
Designers Robin Perkins, Heather Watson, Tony Dowers

2.
Client *Los Angeles International Airports*
Designers Clifford Selbert, Gemma Lawson, Jamie Diersing, Rick Simner

3.
Client *The Jerde Partnership*
Designers Robin Perkins, Greg Welsh

4.
Client *Diamond Technology Partners*
Creative Director Jane Kosstrin
Designer Mark Maltais

5.
Client *Digital Navigation*
Designer Susan Lesko

6.
Client *Crunch*
Creative Director Jane Kosstrin
Designer Robert Wong

7.
Client *Open Market, Inc.*
Designers Mike Balint, Clifford Selbert

8.
Client *The Kitchen*
Creative Director Jane Kosstrin
Designer David Buddenhagen

9.
Client *Premise Communication System*
Designer Randall Herrera

10.
Client *The Jerde Partnership*
Designers Robin Perkins, John Lutz, Mike Balint, Greg Welsh

11.
Client *Integrated Network Concepts*
Designers Susan Lesko, Randall Herrera

12.
Client *Salem State College*
Designers Clifford Selbert, Robert Merk

13.
Client *Komar*
Creative Director Jane Kosstrin
Designer David Lee

14.
Client *Diamond Technology Partners*
Creative Director Jane Kosstrin
Designer Mark Maltais

15.
Client *Viacom, New Media*
Creative Director Jane Kosstrin
Designer Reinhard Knolebelspies

1.

2.

3.

4.

5.

6.

7.

8.

The PRINT Company

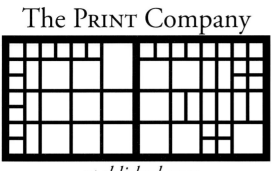

established 1971

9.

ClickCom

10.

11.

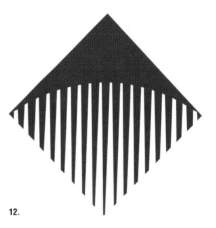

12.

BARRPictures

13.

14.

15.

PRIMETECH

1.

ANDREW HUNT PHOTOGRAPHY

2.

3.

4.

IMAGEMAKER
CD-R DUPLICATION SYSTEM

5.

THE VISUAL GROUP
graphic communications

6.

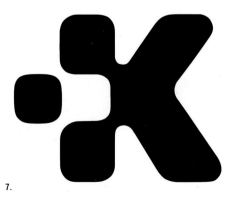

7.

CABAÑA
PALO ALTO

8.

9.

10.

11.

12.

13.

14.

15.

1, 2, 4, 5, 6, 8, 9, 10, 13, 14
 Design Firm **The Visual Group**
3, 7, 11, 12, 15
 Design Firm **Eskil Ohlsson Associates Inc.**

1.
 Client *Primetech, Inc.*
 Designers Ark Stein, Bill Mifsud

2.
 Client *Andrew Hunt Photography*
 Designer Ark Stein

3.
 Client *F.T. & M. Inc.*
 Designer Eskil Ohlsson

4.
 Client *Taxi Service Co.*
 Designer Ark Stein

5.
 Client *Microtech Co. Inc.*
 Designer Ark Stein

6.
 Client *The Visual Group*
 Designers Ark Stein, Vadim Goretsky

7.
 Client *Kroma Lithographers, Inc.*
 Designer Eskil Ohlsson

8.
 Client *Cabaña Hotel*
 Designer Ark Stein

9.
 Client *Zero G Software*
 Designers Ark Stein, Bill Mifsud

10.
 Client *To The Point*
 Designer Ark Stein

11.
 Client *Cline, Davis & Mann Inc. (Proworx)*
 Designers Andy Moore, Eskil Ohlsson

12.
 Client *Mercantile Leasing Corp.*
 Designer Eskil Ohlsson

13.
 Client *Evotech Co. Inc.*
 Designer Ark Stein

14.
 Client *Sentius Corporation*
 Designers Bill Mifsud, Ark Stein

15.
 Client *T. Rowe Price*
 Designer Eskil Ohlsson

1.

2.

3.

COMFORTS

SAN ANSELMO, CALIFORNIA

4.

5.

ICE CREAM

6.

7.

(all)
Design Firm **Axion Design Inc.**
1.
   Client   *Teledyne*
2.
   Client   *Sara Lee*
3.
   Client   *Memtek*
4.
   Client   *Comforts*
5.
   Client   *Clorox*
6.
   Client   *Dreyer's*
7.
   Client   *Jimmy Dean*

(opposite)
   Client   *Pharmavite*
   Design Firm **Axion Design Inc.**

c o n

1.

LOFTIN
& COMPANY
PRINTERS

2.

3.

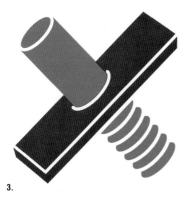

TROY SYSTEMS

4.

SYNETICS

5.

6.

TechnologyChambers

7.

LA PIÑATA

8.

148

9.

10.

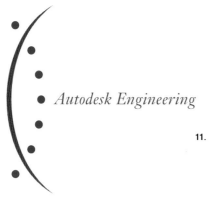

Autodesk Engineering

11.

12.

STACKS'

13.

14.

15.

1		
Design Firm	**R. Morris Design**	
2, 6, 7, 14		
Design Firm	**Steve Thomas Marketing Communications**	
3, 8, 9, 11-13		
Design Firm	**Bruce Yelaska Design**	
4, 5		
Design Firm	**Grafik Communications, Ltd**	
10		
Design Firm	**Heckler Associates**	
15		
Design Firm	**Axion Design Inc.**	

1.
Client   *Icon Design*
Designer   Rock Morris
2.
Client   *Loftin & Company*
Designer   Steve Thomas
3.
Client   *Autodesk Engineering*
Designers   Bruce Yelaska, John Seminario
4.
Client   *Troy Systems*
Designers   David Collins, Judy Kirpich
5.
Client   *Synetics*
Designers   Kristin Moore, Judy Kirpich

6.
Client   *Fred Wilkerson*
Designer   Steve Thomas
7.
Client   *Technology Chambers*
Designer   Steve Thomas
8.
Client   *La Pinata*
Designer   Bruce Yelaska
9.
Client   *Cafe Toma*
Designers   Bruce Yelaska
10.
Client   *Starbucks Coffee Co.*
Designer   Terry Heckler
11.
Client   *Autodesk Engineering*
Designer   Bruce Yelaska
12.
Client   *The University of California*
Designer   Bruce Yelaska
13.
Client   *Stacks'*
Designer   Bruce Yelaska
14.
Client   *Metasys*
Designers   Steve Thomas
15.
Client   *Franzia*

Inland Entertainment
C O R P O R A T I O N

1.

FIRSTWORLD™
C O M M U N I C A T I O N S

2.

3.

4.

ANIKA
T H E R A P E U T I C S

5.

BIG DEAHL

6.

WILDLIFE

7.

1-4, 6, 7
Design Firm **Mires Design, Inc.**
5
Design Firm **Ellis Pratt Design**
1.
Client   *Inland Entertainment Corporation*
Designers   José Serrano, John Ball,
         Miguel Perez
Illustrator   Miguel Perez
2.
Client   *First World Communications*
Designers   John Ball, Miguel Perez,
         Kathy Carpentier-Moore
3.
Client   *Nike Inc.*
Designers   John Ball, Miguel Perez
Illustrator   Tracy Sabin

4.
Client   *Airtouch Cellular*
Designers   Scott Mires, Deborah Hom
5.
Client   *Anika Therapeutics*
Designers   Elaine Pratt, Vernon Ellis
6.
Client   *Big Deahl*
Designers   José Serrano, Miguel Perez
7.
Client   *California Center for the Arts*
Designers   John Ball, Gale Spitzley
(opposite)
Client   *Green Field Paper Company*
Design Firm   **Mires Design, Inc.**
Designers   José Serrano, Miguel Perez
Illustrator   Dan Thoner

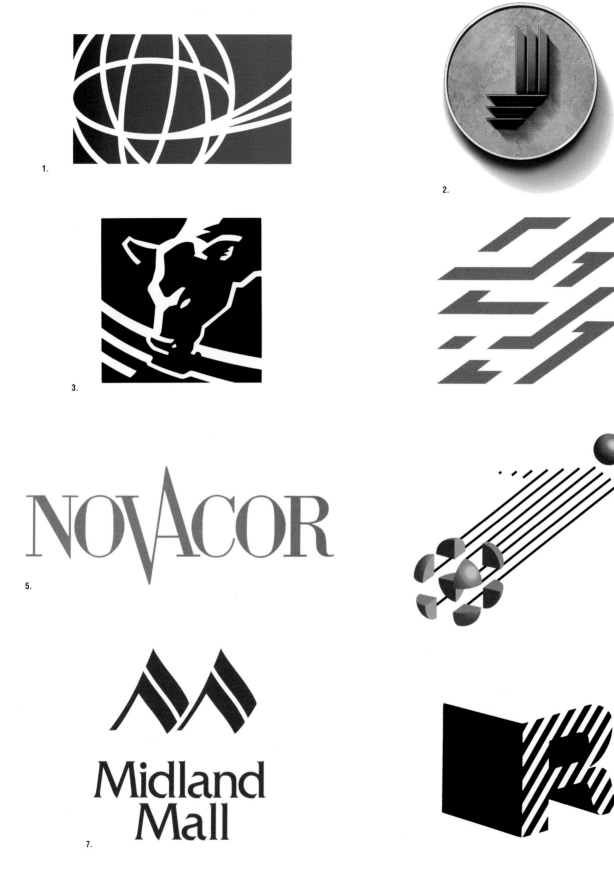

1.

2.

3.

4.

NOVACOR

5.

6.

Midland
Mall

7.

8.

152

9.

10.

11.

12.

13.

14.

Northfield
Mall

15.

1, 4, 6, 10, 13, 14
   Design Firm **Joe Miller's Company**
2, 3, 7-9, 11, 12, 15
   Design Firm **Herip Design Associates**
5
   Design Firm **Burson Marstellar/
                Joe Miller's Company**

1.
   Client   *Quantum*
   Designers Joe Miller, Mai Nguyen
2.
   Client   *The Richard E. Jacobs Group*
   Designer John R. Menter
3.
   Client   *Indian Creek Farm*
   Designer Walter M. Herip
4.
   Client   *Grand/Abacus Business Forms*
   Designer Joe Miller
5.
   Client   *Novacor*
   Designer Joe Miller
6.
   Client   *Tandem*
   Designers Joe Miller, Michael Lauretano

7.
   Client   *The Richard E. Jacobs Group*
   Designer John R. Menter
8.
   Client   *Ronald H. Rasmussen Assoc.*
   Designer Walter M. Herip
9.
   Client   *Herip Design Associates*
   Designer Walter M. Herip
10.
   Client   *Quantum*
   Designers Joe Miller, Mai Nguyen
11.
   Client   *Illes Construction Company*
   Designers Walter M. Herip, John R. Menter
12.
   Client   *John D. May, Jr., Inc.*
   Designer Walter M. Herip
13.
   Client   *Rocket Productions*
   Designer Joe Miller
14.
   Client   *Shade*
   Designer Joe Miller
15.
   Client   *The Richard E. Jacobs Group*
   Designer Walter M. Herip, John R. Menter

DENVER BUFFALO COMPANY

1.

Kootenai
Medical
Center

2.

DANIELS
&ASSOCIATES

3.

ANTHEM HOMES

4.

Hanifen, Imhoff
Clearing Corp.

5.

FISERV CORRESPONDENT
SERVICES, INC.

6.

THE ISLAND CLUB

Great Exuma · Bahamas

7.

*Commercial
Federal*

8.

CONCENTRA
Medical Centers

9.

FirsTier

10.

Golf Lodging™

11.

AMQUEST
BANK

12.

VANGUARD
AIRLINES

13.

YALE-NEW HAVEN HOSPITAL

14.

A VISION OF THE FUTURE

15.

(all)
Design Firm **Matrix International Assoc., Ltd.**

1.
Client — Denver Buffalo Co.
Designers — Duane Wiens, Dan Funk

2.
Client — Kootenai Medical Center
Designers — Duane Wiens, Matt Scharf

3.
Client — Daniels & Associates, Inc.
Designers — Duane Wiens, Carl Baden

4.
Client — Anthem Homes, Inc.
Designers — Duane Wiens, Dan Funk

5.
Client — Hanifen Imhoff, Inc.
Designers — Duane Wiens, Carl Baden

6.
Client — Fiserv Correspondent Services, Inc.
Designers — Duane Wiens, Carl Baden

7.
Client — The Bahama Club
Designers — Duane Wiens, Dan Funk

8.
Client — Commercial Federal Bank, Inc.
Designers — Duane Wiens, Carl Baden

9.
Client — Concentra Medical Centers
Designers — Duane Wiens, Dan Funk

10.
Client — FirsTier Financial Corp.
Designers — Duane Wiens, Carl Baden

11.
Client — Golf Lodging LLC
Designers — Duane Wiens, Dan Funk, Margo Newman

12.
Client — Amquest Financial Corp.
Designers — Duane Wiens, Carl Baden

13.
Client — Vanguard Airlines
Designers — Duane Wiens, Carl Baden

14.
Client — Yale New Haven Health
Designers — Duane Wiens, Margo Newman

15.
Client — Daniels & Associates
Designers — Duane Wiens, Dan Funk

BARCLAY TOWERS

1.

2.

3.

CME

4.

5.

The Children's Hospital

THE KOSSOW CORPORATION

6.

7.

8.

156

9.

Vail Associates, Inc.

10.

plan west

11.

12.

14.

YMCA OF THE ROCKIES

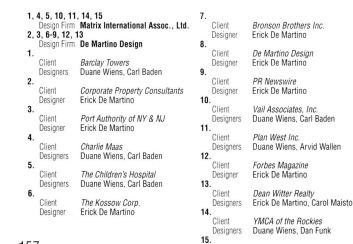

THE BAHAMA CLUB

13.

15.

Rock Creek

Aluminum

1.

STEEPLE

CHASE

2.

SUMMIT

CONSULTING

GROUP

3.

ULTRA/FAB

4.

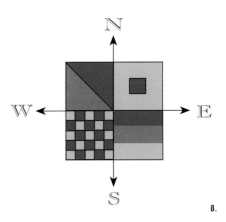

SUMMIT PARTNERS

5.

Global Cinema

N E T W O R K

6.

VIKING

7.

N

W ← → E

S

8.

9.

10.

11.

12.

14.

13.

15.

1, 2, 4, 9, 14
Design Firm **Design Associates, Inc.**
3, 5, 6, 8, 10
Design Firm **Hess Design, Inc.**
7, 11-13, 15
Design Firm **MacVicar Design & Communications**

1.
Client   *Rock Creek Aluminum*
Designer Don Borger
2.
Client   *Adpro*
Designer Don Borger
3.
Client   *Summit Consulting Group*
4.
Client   *Marketing Sciences America*
Designer Don Borger
5.
Client   *Summit Partners*
Designer Kim Daly
6.
Client   *General Cinema*
Designer Kim Daly
7.
Client   *Viking*
Designer Christopher Duerk

8.
Client   *IRSA—International Raquet Sports Association*
Designer Karyn Goba
9.
Client   *Design Associates, Inc.*
Designer Don Borger
10.
Client   *Pure, Inc.*
11.
Client   *Association of Universities for Research in Astronomy, Inc.*
Designer William A. Gordon
12.
Client   *Newsletter Services, Inc.*
Designer William A. Gordon
13.
Client   *Reality Technologies, Inc.*
Designer Cathy Broadwell
14.
Client   *Johnston Metal Industries*
Designer Don Borger
15.
Client   *Independent Insurance Agents of America, Inc.*
Designer William A. Gordon

1.

SPACE AGE
space age advertising, inc.

2.

BELL-CARTER
OLIVE CO.
LINDSAY · PRIVATE LABEL · FOODSERVICE

3.

SAN FRANCISCO FOOD BANK
Feeding the programs that feed the people

4.

The Learning Company®
For Greater Knowledge

5.

CriticalPath SM

6.

VSP
AMERICA'S FIRST CHOICE FOR EYECARE SM

7.

8.

consensus
H E A L T H

9.

10.

LASER & SKIN AESTHETICS CENTER

11.

REEL CITY
P R O D U C T I O N S

12.

pandesic™

13.

14.

HOLLAND
BROTHERS™
HANDMADE IN AMERICA

15.

1.

2.

**CLOTHES
THE DEAL**

3.

WCBF

4.

5.

6.

7.

(all)
Design Firm **Shimokochi/Reeves**
1.
Client   *United Way of America*
Art Director   Saul Bass
Designers   Saul Bass, Mamoru Shimokochi
Artists   Art Goodman, Mamoru Shimokochi
Agency   Saul Bass & Assoc.
2.
Client   *Intellisystems*
Designers   Mamoru Shimokochi, Anne Reeves
3.
Client   *Clothes The Deal*
Designers   Mamoru Shimokochi, Anne Reeves
4.
Client   *WCBF—World Children's
               Baseball Fair*
Designers   Mamoru Shimokochi, Anne Reeves

5.
Client   *X-Century*
Designers   Mamoru Shimokochi, Anne Reeves
6.
Client   *Warp, Inc.*
Designers   Mamoru Shimokochi, Anne Reeves
7.
Client   *United Airlines*
Art Directors Saul Bass, Art Goodman
Designers   Saul Bass, Art Goodman, Mamoru
               Shimokochi, Vince Carra
Agency   Saul Bass & Assoc.
(opposite)
Client   *TBS—Tokyo Broadcasting System*
Design Firm   **Shimokochi/Reeves**
Designers   Mamoru Shimokochi, Anne Reeves

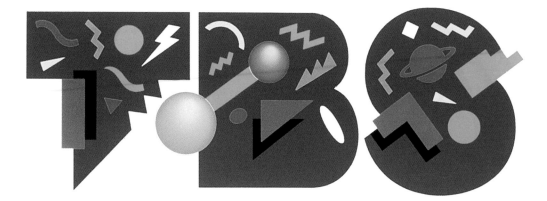

Tokyo Broadcasting System

FOOD & FUN

FUN·JUNCTION

FOREVER!

1.

2. v e t r a

3.

HERNDON SQUARE II

4.

5.

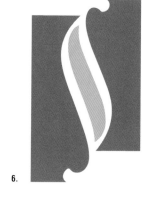

6.

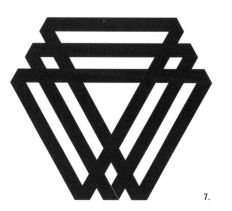

TriNet

8.

7.

166

Women for Women 9.

10.

DULLES TECH CENTER 11.

12.

ONE FAIR OAKS 13.

TM

TIMEBRIDGE
TECHNOLOGIES

14.

15.

(all)
Design Firm **Fuller Designs, Inc.**

1.
Client *Fun Junction*
Designer Doug Fuller

2.
Client *Vetra*
Designer Doug Fuller

3.
Client *Campaign on Clinical Depression*
Designers Doug Fuller, Aaron Taylor

4.
Client *Trammell Crow Company*
Designers Doug Fuller, Karen Yenchi

5.
Client *Fuller Designs, Inc.*
Designer Doug Fuller

6.
Client *Signature Group*
Designer Doug Fuller

7.
Client *Virginia Integrated Physicians*
Designer Doug Fuller

8.
Client *TriNet Healthcare Systems*
Designer Doug Fuller

9.
Client *Women for Women*
Designer Doug Fuller

10.
Client *Premium Distributors*
Designer Aaron Taylor

11.
Client *Trammell Crow Company*
Designer Doug Fuller

12.
Client *Marhoefer Communications*
Designer Doug Fuller

13.
Client *Trammell Crow Company*
Designer Doug Fuller

14.
Client *TimeBridge Technologies*
Designer Aaron Taylor

15.
Client *International Society for Performance Improvement*
Designer Aaron Taylor

1.

2. gatti·town

3. TM

4. SYLVESTRE
FRANC
SALON

5.

6. BECKLEY IMPORTS

7. CENTURY ·CLUB·

8. CTM

9.

10.

PINNACLE

11.

20TH CENTURY DESIGN

12.

13.

14.   P R O D U C T I O N S

15.

1, 4, 10			
Design Firm	**Misha Design Studio**	**7.**	
2		Client	*National Travelers Life "Century Club"*
Design Firm	**Sibley/Peteet Design**	Designer	John Sayles
3, 6-9, 11-13		**8.**	
Design Firm	**Sayles Graphic Design**	Client	*Cutler Travel Marketing*
5, 15		Designer	John Sayles
Design Firm	**Mervil Paylor Design**	**9.**	
14		Client	*Java Joes*
Design Firm	**Fuller Designs, Inc.**	Designer	John Sayles
1.		**10.**	
Client	*Russian-American Music Association*	Client	*Yury's Piano / Boston*
Designer	Michael Lenn	Designer	Michael Lenn
2.		**11.**	
Client	*Mr. Gatti's Restaurants*	Client	*Berlin Packaging "Pinnacle"*
Designers	Rex Peteet	Designer	John Sayles
3.		**12.**	
Client	*Consolidated Correctional Food Services*	Client	*Christine's 20th Century Furnishings*
Designer	John Sayles	Designer	John Sayles
4.		**13.**	
Client	*Sylvestre Franc/Hair Salon*	Client	*Raccoon River Brewing Company*
Designer	Michael Lenn	Designer	John Sayles
5.		**14.**	
Client	*The Democratic Cause*	Client	*Ventana Productions*
Designer	Mervil M. Paylor	Designer	Aaron Taylor
6.		**15.**	
Client	*Beckley Imports*	Client	*First Union, Community Reinvestment*
Designer	John Sayles	Designer	Mervil M. Paylor

1.

APPLIED
GLOBAL
UNIVERSITY

2.

3.

4. **ITCN**
SOLUTIONS FOR EMBEDDED SYSTEMS INTEGRATION

ARACHNID
design

5.

6. A S K S

MainSail
7. PRODUCTION SERVICES INC.

eLLIOTT®
TOOL TECHNOLOGIES

8.

170

 **Wireless Financial Services** 9.

 STRUCT-A-LITE 10.

 ATCC 11.

12.

 Anergen 13.

ec**o**mat 14.

 McCAULEY™
15.

1
Design Firm **Bruce Yelaska Design**
2, 6, 13
Design Firm **Howry Design Associates**
3, 12
Design Firm **MediaConcept Corporation**
4, 7, 8, 10, 15
Design Firm **Nova Creative Group, Inc.**
5
Design Firm **Stephanie Cunningham**
9, 11, 14
Design Firm **Stephen Loges Graphic Design**

1.
Client   *The Gauntlett Group*
Designer   Bruce Yelaska
2.
Client   *Applied Global University*
Art Director   Jill Howry
Designer   Todd Richards
3.
Client   *The Boston Plan for Excellence
in the Public Schools*
Designer   Chris O'Toole
4.
Client   *ITCN*
Designer   Tim O'Hare
5.
Client   *Arachnid Design*
Designer   Stephanie Cunningham

6.
Client   *Applied Strategic
Knowledge Solutions*
Art Director   Jill Howry
Designer   Todd Richards
7.
Client   *MainSail Production Services*
Designer   Tim O'Hare
8.
Client   *Elliott Tool Technologies*
Designer   Greg Vennerholm
9.
Client   *Wireless Financial Services, Inc.*
Designer   Stephen Loges
10.
Client   *Struct-A-Lite*
Designer   Tim O'Hare
11.
Client   *ATCC
(American Type Culture Collection)*
Designer   Stephen Loges
12.
Client   *Schmid*
Designer   Paul Beaulieu
13.
Client   *Anergen, Inc.*
Art Director   Jill Howry
Designer   Gayle Steinbeigle
14.
Client   *Ecofranchising, Inc,*
Designer   Stephen Loges
15.
Client   *McCauley Propellers*
Designer   Dwayne Swormstedt

171

1.

2.

WORLDESIGN

3.

MACDONALD CONSTRUCTION

4.

5.

|m|a|h|a|r|a|m|

6.

7.

1, 2
Design Firm **Ross West Design**
3, 5-7
Design Firm **Matsumoto Incorporated**
4
Design Firm **Icon Imagery**
1.
Client *Universal Bar*
Designer Ross West
2.
Client *Victory Coffee*
Designer Ross West
3.
Client *Worldesign Foundation*
Designer Takaaki Matsumoto
4.
Client *MacDonald Construction*
Designer Ross West

5.
Client *Sazaby, Inc.*
Designer Takaaki Matsumoto
6.
Client *Maharam*
Designer Takaaki Matsumoto
7.
Client *Greenwich Village
Chamber of Commerce*
Designer Takaaki Matsumoto
(opposite)
Client *Okinawa Aquarium*
Design Firm **Matsumoto Incorporated**
Designer Takaaki Matsumoto

172

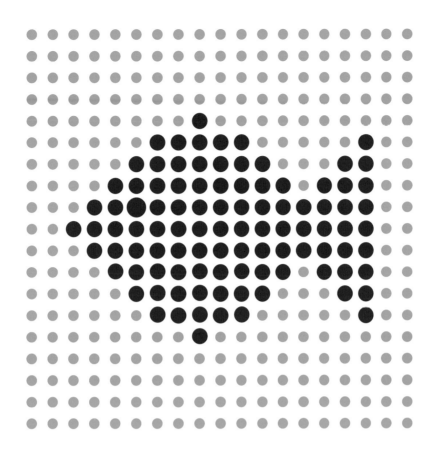

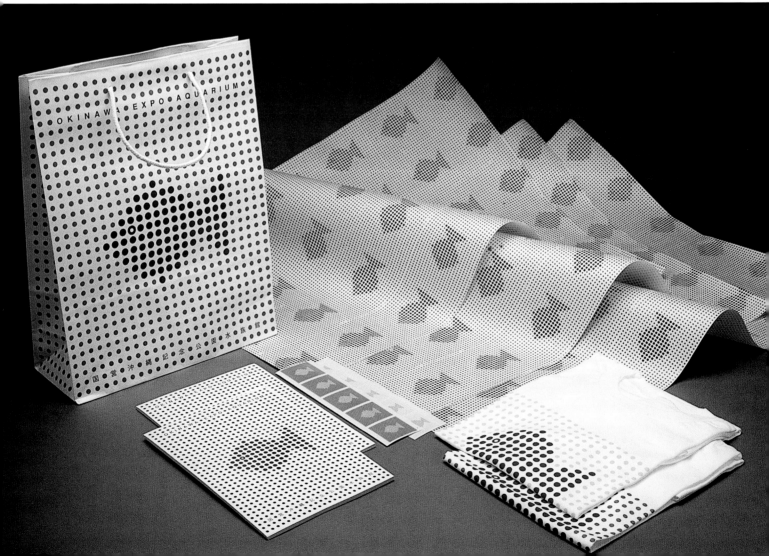

1.

2.

3.

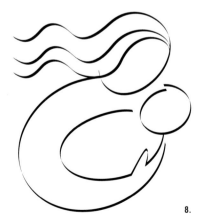

4.

LITHIA

5.

6.

7.

8.

174

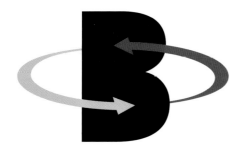

9. B TREE

10.

11.

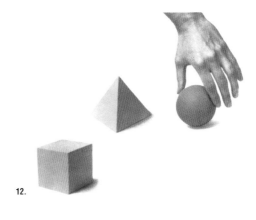

12.

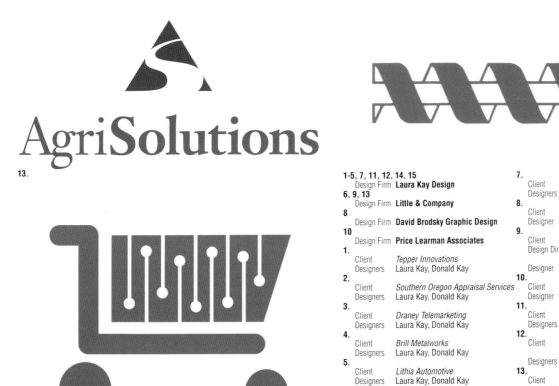

13.

AgriSolutions

14.

15.

1-5, 7, 11, 12, 14, 15
Design Firm **Laura Kay Design**
6, 9, 13
Design Firm **Little & Company**
8
Design Firm **David Brodsky Graphic Design**
10
Design Firm **Price Learman Associates**

1.
Client *Tepper Innovations*
Designers Laura Kay, Donald Kay
2.
Client *Southern Oregon Appraisal Services*
Designers Laura Kay, Donald Kay
3.
Client *Draney Telemarketing*
Designers Laura Kay, Donald Kay
4.
Client *Brill Metalworks*
Designers Laura Kay, Donald Kay
5.
Client *Lithia Automotive*
Designers Laura Kay, Donald Kay
6.
Client *D'Amicao, Metropolitan*
Design Director
  Jim Jackson
Designers Tom Riddle, Garin Ipsen

7.
Client *Thomas Register*
Designers Laura Kay, Donald Kay
8.
Client *St. John's Hospital*
Designer David Brodsky
9.
Client *B-Tree*
Design Director
  Jim Jackson
Designer Scott Sorenson
10.
Client *Jim Dickinson*
Designer Ross West
11.
Client *R & R Transportation Services*
Designers Laura Kay, Donald Kay
12.
Client *Southern Oregon Hand Rehabilitation*
Designers Laura Kay, Donald Kay
13.
Client *AgriSolutions*
Design Director
  Paul Wharton
Designer Tom Riddle
14.
Client *Tara Labs*
Designers Laura Kay, Donald Kay
15.
Client *Thomas Register*
Designers Laura Kay, Donald Kay

Produce**One**

1.

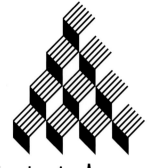

Strategic Accounts

2.

MIAMI VALLEY
WOMEN'S
CENTER

3.

T R E A S U R E D

M O M E N T S

P H O T O G R A P H Y

4.

5.

CHEROKEE
COMMUNICATIONS, INC.

6.

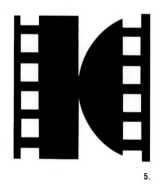

VINEYARD
CHRISTIAN FELLOWSHIP

7.

1-3, 5, 7
  Design Firm **Graphica, Inc.**
4, 6
  Design Firm **Zoe Graphics**
1.
  Client   *Produce One*
  Designer Michael England
2.
  Client   *Square D*
  Designers Al Hidalgo, Mike England
3.
  Client   *Miami Valley Women's Center*
  Designer Michael England
4.
  Client   *Treasured Moments*
  Designers Kim Waters, Kelly Dodds
5.
  Client   *Kim Cooper*
  Designer Jeff Stapleton

6.
  Client   *Cherokee Communications*
  Designers Kathy Pagano, Kim Waters
7.
  Client   *Dayton Vineyard Christian Fellowship*
  Designer Michael England
(opposite)
  Client   *Crown Equipment Corp.*
  Design Firm **Graphica, Inc.**
  Designer Drew Cronenwett

THE CROWN STORE

1.

2.

3.

4.

5.

6.

7.

8.

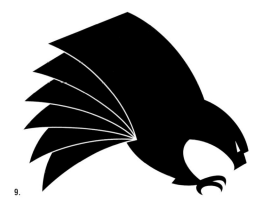

9.

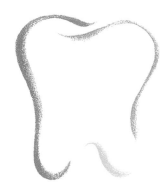

10.

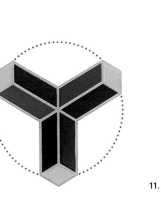

11.

12.

ONE WORLD MUSIC℠

13.

INTELLIGENT BIOCIDES

14.

Tangerine

15.

1.

2.

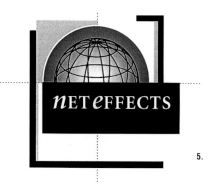

3.

4.

net*e*ffects

5.

COSMED

6.

7.

1, 5-7
Design Firm **Phoenix Creative, St. Louis**
2
Design Firm **Ed Mantels-Seeker**
3, 4
Design Firm **Kiku Obata & Company**
1.
Client   *Shandwick USA/*
            Jewish Federation of St. Louis
Designers   Ed Mantels-Seeker, Eric Thoelke
2.
Client   *The Sambistas*
Designer   Ed Mantels-Seeker
3.
Client   *Barnes West County Hospital -*
            Sports Medicine Center
Designer   Ed Mantels-Seeker

4.
Client   *The Vein Center*
Designer   Ed Mantels-Seeker
5.
Client   *Net Effects*
Designer   Deborah Finkelstein
6.
Client   *CosMed*
Designer   Ed Mantels-Seeker
7.
Client   *Venture Stores*
Designers   Ed Mantels-Seeker, Kathy Wilkinson
(opposite)
Client   *Kaldi's Coffee Roasting*
Design Firm **Phoenix Creative, St. Louis**
Designer   Deborah Finkelstein

1.

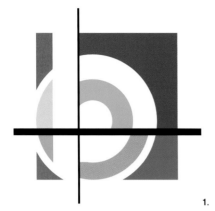

2.

3.

CYPRESS BEND

4.

PATIO CAFE

5.

cbk:milieu

7.

THE MENTORING INSTITUTE

6.

8.

182

TheHernia Institute: 9.

Lil' Britches 10.

11.

COOL BEANS CAFE 12.

13.

LIGHTHOUSE
14.

SPASENSE

15.

1.

2.

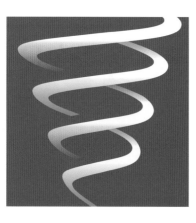

3.

DECATUR
CELEBRATION
THE WORLD'S FAIR OF THE PRAIRIE

4.

5.

Concept
INFORMATION SYSTEMS

6.

THE BLOOD CENTER

7.

8.

9.

10.

11.

12.

13.

FICHT
FUEL INJECTION

14.

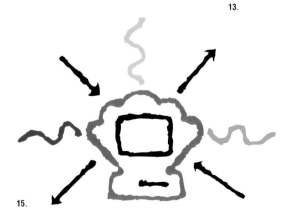

15.

1, 11
Design Firm **Leslie Evans Design**
2, 5, 9, 15
Design Firm **Wet Paper Bag Graphic Design**
3, 8, 10
Design Firm **Parachute, Inc.**
4
Design Firm **David Brodsky Graphic Design**
6
Design Firm **bonatodesign**
7, 14
Design Firm **Design North**
`**12, 13**
Design Firm **Patt Mann Berry Design**

1.
Client *Ducks Unlimited*
Designer Tom Hubbard
2.
Client *PicketFence Community,
GeoCities, Inc.*
Designer Lewis Glaser
3.
Client *Ecolab*
Designer Heather Cooley
4.
Client *Decatur Celebration, Inc.*
Designer David Brodsky
5.
Client *Texas Christian University
Graphic Design Program*
Designer Lewis Glaser

6.
Client *Concept Information Systems*
Designer Donna Bonato Orr
7.
Client *Blood Center*
8.
Client *Galleria*
Designer Cari Johnson
9.
Client *J&D Products, Inc.*
Designer Lewis Glaser
10.
Client *2nd Swing*
Designer Bob Upton
11.
Client *Portland Public Market*
Designers Leslie Evans, Tom Hubbard
12.
Client *Carol & Kanda*
Designer Patt Mann-Berry
13.
Client *NewsHound*
Designer Patt Mann-Berry
14.
Client *Ficht*
Designer Pat Cowan
15.
Client *HyperShell, Inc.*
Designer Lewis Glaser

1.

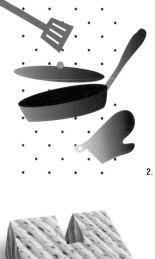

2.

FerExport

MANAGEMENT INC

3.

HEINEN CONSTRUCTION

4.

5.

KVK COMPUTERS

6.

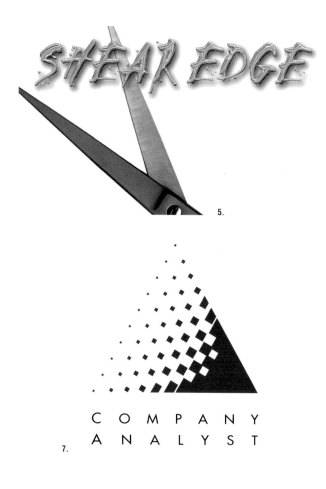

COMPANY
ANALYST

7.

SHEERLUND FORESTS

CHRISTMAS TREE FARM

EST. 1901

8.

C O U R T Y A R D
C A F E

9.

HANNIBAL'S
COFFEE COMPANY

10.

11. **D A T A B O X**

12.

INFO STAR
I N C O R P O R A T E D

13.

A N A L Y S T T O O L™
A PRODUCT OF DISCLOSURE INCORPORATED

Water Spirits Music

14.

15.

1, 4, 5, 14		
Design Firm	**Jefrey Gunion Illustration & Design**	
2		
Design Firm	**Design Moves, Ltd.**	
3, 6-13, 15		
Design Firm	**Lomangino Studio, Inc.**	
1.		
Client	*Silicon Graphics*	
Designers	Frank Doyle, Jefrey Gunion	
2.		
Client	*Association of Home Appliance Manufacturers*	
Designers	Laurie Medeiros Freed, Laura Munro	
3.		
Client	*Fer Export Management, Inc.*	
Designer	Lomangino Studio	
4.		
Client	*Heinen Construction*	
Designer	Jefrey Gunion	
5.		
Client	*Shear Edge*	
Designer	Jefrey Gunion	
6.		
Client	*KVK Computers*	
Designer	Arthur Hsu	

7.	
Client	*Disclosure, Inc.*
Designer	Kimberly Pollock
8.	
Client	*Sheerlund Forests*
Designer	Alain Blunt
9.	
Client	*Sheraton Washington Hotel*
Designer	Al Berces
10.	
Client	*Hannibal's Coffee Company*
Designer	Alain Blunt
11.	
Client	*Graphtel*
Designer	Enrique Domenech
12.	
Client	*Infostar, Inc.*
Designer	Alan Blunt
13.	
Client	*Disclosure, Inc.*
Designer	Alain Blunt
14.	
Client	*Water Spirits Music*
Designer	Jefrey Gunion
15.	
Client	*Axiom Training, Inc.*
Designer	Kimberly Pollock

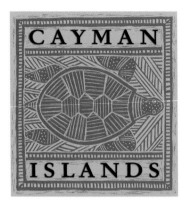

CAYMAN ISLANDS

1.

BROWN DEER PRESS

2.

3.

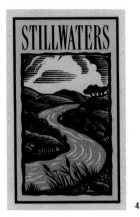

STILLWATERS

4.

5.

BAYONA

6.

THE RIDGE

7.

1, 4
Design Firms **Mires Design, Simple Green**
2
Design Firm **Miriello Grafico**
3
Design Firm **Stoorza, Zeigas & Metzger**
5
Design Firm **Crouch & Naegli**
6
Design Firm **Mires Design**
7
Design Firm **The Flowers Group**

1.
Client   *The Masters Group*
Designers   Mike Brower, Tracy Sabin
Illustrator Tracy Sabin

2.
Client   *Harcourt Brace & Co.*
Designers   Ron Miriello, Tracy Sabin
Illustrator Tracy Sabin

3.
Client   *San Diego Gas & Electric
             (Coyote Division)*
Art Director Craig Fuller
Designer, Illustrator
             Tracy Sabin

4.
Client   *Total Quality Apparel*
Designer   Mike Brower
Illustrator Tracy Sabin

5.
Client   *University of California, San Diego*
Art Directors Jim Crouch, Jim Naegli
Designer, Illustrator
             Tracy Sabin

6.
Client   *McMillin Homes*
Art Director José Serrano
Designer, Illustrator
             Tracy Sabin

7.
Client   *The Ridge*
Designers   Cory Sheehan, Tracy Sabin
Illustrator Tracy Sabin
(opposite)
Client   *McMillin Homes*
Design Firm **Mires Design**
Art Director José Serrano
Designer, Illustrator
             Tracy Sabin

At Cadiz, we've recreated the look of a traditional Spanish country cottage, right down to the wooden garden gates and the red tile roofs. And, more important, we've recaptured the feel with cozy front gardens, enchanting patios, storybook balconies.

1.

2.

3.

WISDOM FROM WHARTON

4.

MONKEY STUDIOS

5.

Bridgewater

6.

7.

CURRENT COMMUNICATIONS

8.

ODYSSEY

9.

10.

BRIDLEWOOD

11.

12.

13.

14.

15.

1, 6, 11
  Design Firm **Knoth & Meads**
2-5, 7-10, 12-15
  Design Firm **Tracy Sabin Graphic Design**
1-10, 12-15
  Designer, Illustrator
              Tracy Sabin
1.
  Client   *McMillin Homes*
  Art Director José Serrano
2.
  Client   *The Miller Band*
  Art Director Jim Welsh
3.
  Client   *Consolite Corporation*
  Art Director Robert Stetzel
4.
  Client   *Chief Executive Magazine*
  Art Director Michael Carpenter
5.
  Client   *Monkey Studios*
  Art Director Russell Sabin
6.
  Client   *McMillin Homes*
  Art Director José Serrano

7.
  Client   *California Beach Co.*
  Art Director Richard Sawyer
8.
  Client   *Current Communications*
  Art Director Alison Hill
9.
  Client   *Harcourt Brace & Co.*
  Art Director Lisa Peters
10.
  Client   *Taylor Guitars*
  Art Director Rita Hoffman
11.
  Client   *McMillin Homes*
  Designer   John Vitro
  Illustrator   Tracy Sabin
12.
  Client   *Turner Entertainment*
  Art Director Alison Hill
13.
  Client   *Turner Entertainment*
  Art Director Lisa Peters
14.
  Client   *Tracy Sabin Graphic Design*
15.
  Client   *Uptown Car Wash*
  Art Director Van Oliver

193

50 YEARS

BRIDGING *the* PACIFIC

1.

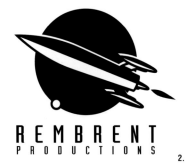

REMBRENT
PRODUCTIONS

2.

3.

GREATER MINNEAPOLIS
CHAMBER OF COMMERCE

4.

KeyWare™

5.

6.

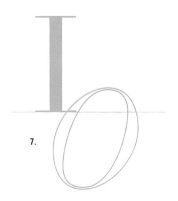

7.

STERNER™

8.

PENTAMERICA PICTURES

9.

LUTHERAN BROTHERHOOD

10.

DigitalMedia L.L.P.

11.

12.

BARLOW RESEARCH ASSOCIATES, INC.

13.

®

14.

THE VENETIAN
Resort·Hotel·Casino ~ Las Vegas

15.

1, 4, 5, 8, 10 - 14
Design Firm **Yamamoto Moss**
2, 3, 6, 9
Design Firm **B.D. Fox & Friends, Advertising**
7, 15
Design Firm **Maddocks & Company**

1.
Client   *Northwest Airlines*
Designer   Brian Adducci
2.
Client   *Rembrent Productions*
Designer   Garrett Burke
3.
Client   *Interplay*
Designer   Garrett Burke
4.
Client   *Greater Minneapolis Chamber of Commerce*
Designer   Keiko Takahashi
5.
Client   *Racotek*
Designers Alan Tse, Chris Cortilet
6.
Client   *The Sci-Fi Channel*
Designer   Rob Biro
7.
Client   *CBI Laboratories, Inc.*
Creative Director, Designer
           Julia Precht

8.
Client   *Sterner Lighting System Inc.*
Designer   Kasey Worrell
9.
Client   *Pentamerica Pictures*
Designer   Rob Biro
10.
Client   *Lutheran Brotherhood*
Designer   Hideki Yamamoto
11.
Client   *Digital Media*
Designer   Alan Tse
12.
Client   *Barlow Research Associates*
Designer   Keiko Takahashi
13.
Designer   Amee Husek
14.
Client   *CNS*
Designers Joan McCarrell, Alan Tse
15.
Client   *The Venetian Hotel & Resort*
Creative Director
           Mary Scott
Designer   Dave Chapple, Amy Hershman
Illustrator Martin Ledvard

INKLINGS DESIGN SM

1.

PLAZA BUILDERS INC.

2.

SIGNAL BANK

3.

AZALEA FILMS

4.

Intelos TM

5.

6.

7.

1, 2
  Design Firm **Inklings Design**
3, 6
  Design Firm **Karen Skunta & Company**
4, 5, 7
  Design Firm **Cadmus Com**
1.
  Client *Inklings Design*
  Designer John Gruber
2.
  Client *Plaza Builders Inc.*
  Designer John Gruber
3.
  Client *Signal Bank*
  Designers Karen L. Hauser, Christopher Oldham, Christopher Suster, Karen A. Skunta

4.
  Client *Azalea Films*
  Designer Brian Thomson
5.
  Client *CFW Communications*
  Designer Brian Thomson
6.
  Client *Whole Health Management Inc.*
  Designers Christopher Suster, Karen A. Skunta
7.
  Client *Gabbert Hood Photography*
  Designer Jess Schaich
(opposite)
  Client *The Freedom Forum*
  Design Firm **Yasumura Assoc., Muts & Joy & Design**
  Designer Gisele Sangiovanni

1.

MTM
FAMILY NETWORK

2.

3.

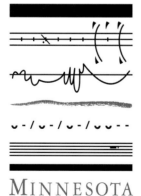

Gillette Children's
Specialty Healthcare

4.

Guthrie Theater

5.

The
Fisher's
Net

6.

MINNESOTA
STATE ARTS BOARD

7.

Discovery begins here

8.

9.

10.

11.

12.

SUMMIT
E N T E R T A I N M E N T

13.

14.

15.

Concordia
UNIVERSITY·SAINT PAUL

199

1 - 3, 10 -13		
Design Firm	**B.D. Fox & Friends, Advertising**	
4 - 9, 14, 15		
Design Firm	**Yamamoto Moss**	
1.		
Client	*Warner Bros.*	
Designers	Bill Garland, Lee MacLeod	
2.		
Client	*MTM Television Distribution*	
Designer	Cindy Luck	
3.		
Client	*Big Entertainment*	
Designer	Garrett Burke	
4.		
Client	*Gillette Children's Hospital*	
Designer	Kasey Worrell	
5.		
Designer	Brian Adducci	
6.		
Client	*Lutheran Brotherhood*	
Designer	Alan Tse	

7.	
Client	*Minnesota State Arts Board*
Designer	Julie Szamocki
8.	
Designer	Brain Adducci
9.	
Client	*TARGET Greatland*
Designer	Brian Adducci
10.	
Client	*Sega of America*
Designer	Garrett Burke
11.	
Client	*Republic Pictures*
Designer	Cindy Luck
12.	
Client	*Big Entertainment*
Designers	Rob Biro, Mike Bryan
13.	
Client	*Summit Entertainment*
14.	
Client	*Green Mountain Energy Partners*
Designers	Kasey Worrell, Keiko Takahashi
15.	
Client	*Concordia College*
Designer	Brian Adducci

1.

2.

3.

FIRSTLIGHT

4.

Stillwaters™

5.

MUNICIPAL·FLOW
—PROMOTIONS—

6.

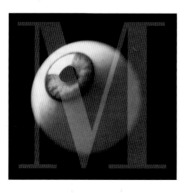

7.

NOMADS

8.

202

9.

10.

11.

12.

GREENING
EARTH
SOCIETY

JPATS
MB339·LOCKHEED·AERMACCHI·HUGHES

13.

14.

LOCK
ON
TECHNOLOGY ™

15.

1, 7 - 10, 12
   Design Firm **Signal Communications**
2 - 6
   Design Firm **Simple Green Design**
11
   Design Firm **Pirman Communications**
13 - 15
   Design Firm **B.D. Fox & Friends, Advertising**

1.
   Client   *Picture Factory*
   Designer Scott Severson
2.
   Client   *Department of Power*
   Designer Mike Brower
3.
   Client   *Department of Power*
   Designers Mike Brower, Russ Acol-Scott
4.
   Client   *Total Quality Apparel*
   Designer Mike Brower
5.
   Client   *Total Quality Apparel*
   Designer Mike Brower
6.
   Client   *Municipal Flow Promotions*
   Designer Russ Acol-Scott

7.
   Client   *Dan Mullen Photography*
   Designer Scott Severson
8.
   Client   *Nomads*
   Designer JJ Chrystal
9.
   Client   *Photo Effects*
   Designer Scott Severson
10.
   Client   *Starland Cafe*
   Designer Scott Severson
11.
   Client   *Pirman Communications*
   Designer Brian Pirman
12.
   Client   *Greening Earth Society*
   Designer Scott Severson
13.
   Client   *Lockheed*
   Designer Rob Biro
14.
   Client   *Warner Bros.*
   Designers Tom Nikosey, Garrett Burke
15.
   Client   *Sega of America*
   Designer Cindy Luck

1.

CHARLOTTE

2.

3.

PILCH

4.

5.

UNCCHARLOTTE

6.

SEQUOIA
T E C H N O L O G Y

7.

1, 7
Design Firm **Via Design Inc.**
2 - 6
Design Firm **Design/Joe Sonderman**
1.
  Client   *Biodynamics, Inc.*
  Designer   Lee Perrault
2.
  Client   *City of Charlotte*
  Designers   Yasu Taguchi, Mary Head,
              Joe Sonderman
3.
  Client   *The Hilton Head Co.*
  Designer   Joe Sonderman
4.
  Client   *Pilch, Inc.*
  Designers   Joe Sonderman, Tim Gilland

5.
  Client   *Charlotte Motor Speedway*
  Designer   Joe Sonderman
6.
  Client   *UNC Charlotte*
  Designers   Tim Gilland, Joe Sonderman,
              Andy Crews
7.
  Client   *Sequoia Technology*
  Designers   Lee Perrault, George Holt
(opposite)
  Client   *Steuben Child Care Project*
  Design Firm **Michael Orr + Associates, Inc.**
  Designers   Michael R. Orr + Associates

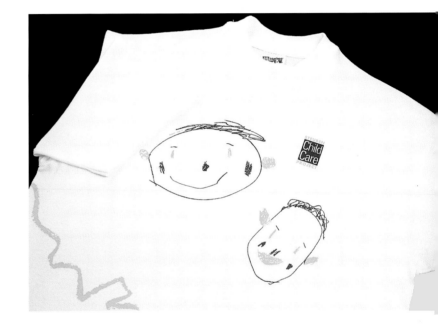

1.

2.

3.

P O L A R I S

V E N T U R E   P A R T N E R S

4.

5.

6.

7.

8.

PEAPOD PROPERTIES LTD.

9.

10.

ERNST & YOUNG LLP

entyron

11.

13.

14.

15.

1.

BROCATO®

An American Attitude For Hair™

2.

3.

4.

5.

6.

7.

(all)
Design Firm **DSI/LA**

1.
Client — *Louisiana Electric Cooperatives, Inc.*
Designers — Hoa Van Vu, Rod Parker

2.
Client — *Brocato International*
Designers — Todd Palisi, Rod Parker

3.
Client — *DSI/LA*
Designers — Pat Vining, Carol Caulfield, Todd Palisi

4.
Client — *Reily Electrical*
Designer — Bryan Murphy

5.
Client — *Walsh Cinematography*
Designers — Rod Parker, Tim Hope

6.
Client — *Louisiana Health Services, LLC*
Designer — Todd Palisi

7.
Client — *Premier Bank*
Designers — Tim Hope, Bryan Murphy

(opposite)
Client — *Leshner Inc.*
Design Firm — **Muts & Joy & Design**
Designers — Katherine Hames, Gisele Sangiovanni

MARK PETRICOFF
CHIEF EXECUTIVE OFFICER

LESHNER™

LESHNER CORPORATION
1010 EATON AVENUE
HAMILTON, OH 45013

TEL 513 868 3500
FAX 513 868 1549

1.

2.

JOHN SCHERER & ASSOCIATES

Transforming the world at work

3.

SPOKANE
VALLEY
CHAMBER
OF COMMERCE

4.

L A N D
EXPRESSIONS LLC

5.

AMERICAN INDIAN
COMMUNITY
CENTER

6.

[cyberjava]
internet services

7.

8.

EAGLE RIDGE

9.

Spokane Airport System

10.

11.

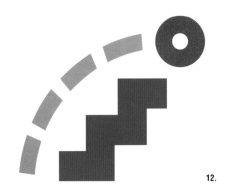

12.

TIGERS®

SUCCESS SERIES

13.

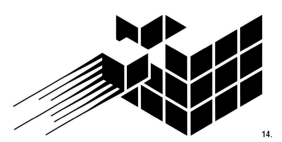

14.

PARAGON
CAPITAL

15.

1 - 7, 9, 10, 13, 14
Design Firm **Klundt + Hosmer Design Assoc.**
8, 11, 12, 15
Design Firm **Crocker Inc.**

1.
Client — *City of Spokane*
Designers — Darin Klundt, Rick Hosmer, Brian Gage

2.
Client — *Riverfront Park*
Designers — Darin Klundt, Rick Hosmer,

3.
Client — *John Scherer & Associates*
Designers — Darin Klundt, Rick Hosmer, Brian Gage

4.
Client — *Spokane Valley Chamber of Commerce*
Designers — Darin Klundt, Amy Gunter, Rick Hosmer

5.
Client — *Land Expressions*
Designers — Darin Klundt, Brian Gage

6.
Client — *American Indian Community Center*
Designers — Darin Klundt, Rick Hosmer, Brian Gage

7.
Designer — Brian Gage

8.
Client — *Mt. Sinai Children's Center*
Designer — Bruce Crocker

9.
Client — *Genstar*
Designers — Darin Klundt, Brian Gage

10.
Client — *Spokane Airport System*
Designers — Darin Klundt, Rick Hosmer, Brian Gage

11.
Client — *Steve Marsel Studio*
Designer — Bruce Crocker

12.
Client — *National Sports Center for Disabled*
Designer — Bruce Crocker

13.
Client — *Tigers Success Series*
Designers — Darin Klundt, Rick Hosmer, Brian Gage

14.
Client — *Personnel Unlimited*
Designers — Darin Klundt, Rick Hosmer

15.
Client — *Paragon Capital*
Designer — Bruce Crocker

211

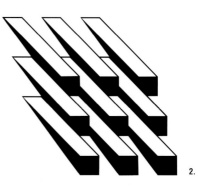

1.

2.

3.

4.

BODYSCAPES

5.

6.

7.

8.

9.

10.

11.

12.

13.

14.

15.

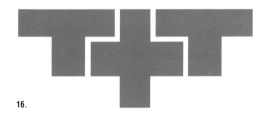

16.

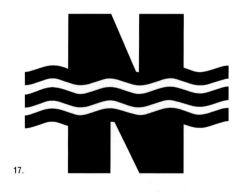

17.

1, 3, 4, 7, 12, 15
Design Firm **Vance Wright Adams & Associates**

2, 5, 6, 8, 9, 11, 13, 14, 17
Design Firm **Essex Two / Chicago**

10
Design Firm **arismendi KNOX, Ltd.**

16
Design Firm **T+T Design**

1.
Client   *Pittsburgh Penguins*
Designers   Gary Adams, Karen Burns

2.
Client   *Paslode, Inc*
Designers   Joseph Michael Essex,
            Nancy Denney Essex

3.
Client   *Coury Financial Services, Inc.*
Designers   Gary Adams, Susan Borach

4.
Client   *Pittsburgh Civic Arena*
Designer   Karen Burns

5.
Client   *Bodyscapes, Inc.*
Designer   Nancy Denney Essex

6.
Client   *The Fulcrum Network, Inc.*
Designers   Nataile Mills Bontumasi,
            Joseph Michael Essex

7.
Client   *Pace Entertainment Group*
Designers   Susan Borach, Karen Burns

8.
Client   *Spiegel, Inc.*
Designers   Joseph Michael Essex,
            Nancy Denney Essex

9.
Client   *Motorola, Inc.*
Designers   Joseph Michael Essex,
            Nancy Denney Essex

10.
Client   *Picnic Works*
Designers   Rafael A. Holguin, Susan K. Hodges

11.
Client   *National Surgery Centers, Inc.*
Designers   Joseph Michael Essex,
            Nancy Denney Essex

12.
Client   *Pittsburgh Sports Festival*
Designer   Paul Schifino

13.
Client   *Johnson Products, Inc. and the
            Dr. Martin Luther King Foundation*
Designers   Joseph Michael Essex,
            Nancy Denney Essex

14.
Client   *The Weaving Workshop, Inc.*
Designers   Joseph Michael Essex,
            Nancy Denney Essex

15.
Client   *Mountaineer Race Track
            & Resort*
Designer   Gary Adams

16.
Client   *T+T Design*
Designers   Theodore C. Alexander, Jr.,
            Therese Alexander

17.
Client   *River North Association*
Designers   Joseph Michael Essex,
            Nancy Denney Essex

1. DISCOUNT CLEANERS ™

2. PRISM

3. InterLan Networks ™

4. RED TOMATO

5. CLINICAL INFORMATION CONSULTANTS, INC.

6. HIGH SIERRA ® PASSPORT TO ADVENTURE

7. Air Quality Laboratory ™

8. RICE PAPER

9. INTERNETsource

CAP
Solutions Compounded

10.

11. Keller Groves, Inc.

12.

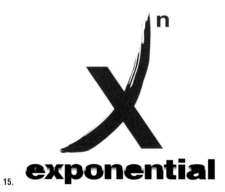

13.

14.

exponential

15.

16.

TRIANGLE MLS
MULTIPLE LISTING SERVICES

17.

1, 3, 5, 7, 17
Design Firm **Polloni Design**
Designer Alberto Polloni
2, 4, 6, 11, 12, 13, 14
Design Firm **JOED Design Inc.**
Designer Edward Rebek
8, 10, 15, 16
Design Firm **Russell Leong Design**
Designer Russell Leong
9
Design Firm **Maddocks & Company**
1.
Client *Discount Cleaners*
2.
Client *Prism Systems*
3.
Client *Interlan Networks*
4.
Client *Red Tomato Inc.*
5.
Client *Clinical Information Consultants, Inc.*

6.
Client *H.Bernbaum Import Export Co.*
7.
Client *Air Quality Laboratory*
8.
Client *Rice Paper, Inc.*
9.
Client *Internet Source*
Creative Director
Mary Scott
Designers Winnie Li, Paul Farris
10.
Client *Central Avenue Pharmacy*
11.
Client *Keller Groves Inc.*
12.
Client *Candle Corporation of America*
13.
Client *American Heart Association*
14.
Client *TradeLink America, Inc.*
15.
Client *Exponential Technologies, Inc.*
16.
Client *GQC Holdings, Inc.*
17.
Client *Triangle MLS*

1.

2.

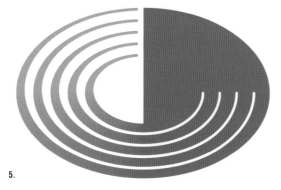

3.

POLLONI DESIGN

4.

5.

6.

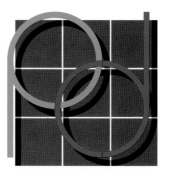

7.

8.

9.

10.

™

11.

12.

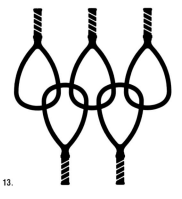

13.

TACO PRONTO

4.

15.

1-3, 5-10, 12-14
Design Firm **Mires Design, Inc.**
4, 11, 15
Design Firm **Polloni Design**

1.
Client   *Taylor Guitars*
Designers   Scott Mires, Miguel Perez
Illustrator   Michael Schwab
Calligrapher Judythe Sieck

2.
Client   *Taylor Guitars*
Designers   Scott Mires, Miguel Perez
Illustrator   Michael Schwab
Calligrapher Judythe Sieck

3.
Client   *Nike Inc.*
Designer   José Serrano
Illustrator   Tracy Sabin

4.
Client   *Polloni Design*
Designer   Alberto Polloni

5.
Client   *Donnelley Enterprise Solutions*
Designers   José Serrano, Miguel Perez

6.
Client   *Tee Shirt Company*
Designer   José Serrano
Illustrator   Dan Thoner

7.
Client   *McGraw Hill Home-Interactive*
Designers   John Ball, Miguel Perez

8.
Client   *M.G. Swing Company*
Designer   Mike Brower
Illustrator   Tracy Sabin

9.
Client   *Taylor Guitars*
Designers   Scott Mires, Miguel Perez
Illustrator   Michael Schwab
Calligrapher Judythe Sieck

10.
Client   *Taylor Guitars*
Designers   Scott Mires, Miguel Perez
Illustrator   Michael Schwab
Calligrapher Judythe Sieck

11.
Client   *The Journey to Teams*
Designers   Alberto Polloni,
              Clina Polloni-Köstner

12.
Client   *Miller Brewing Company*

13.
Client   *Ektelon*
Designer   José Serrano
Illustrator   Dan Thoner

14.
Client   *Taco Pronto*
Designers   John Ball, Scott Mires, Miguel Perez

15.
Client   *Bankers International Trust*
Designer   Alberto Polloni

1.

2.

3.

4.

5.

JABRA

6.

7.

8.

218

9.

10.

11.

12.

13.

14.

15.

1.

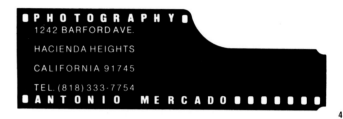

2.

MAGIC
CARPET
BOOKS

3.

PHOTOGRAPHY
1242 BARFORD AVE.
HACIENDA HEIGHTS
CALIFORNIA 91745
TEL. (818) 333-7754
ANTONIO MERCADO

4.

THE BIG ISLAND

Be First With Heart

5.

FUSION

6.

Moore and Associates

7.

8.

1.

DEEP ELLUM 2.

3.

4.

5.

6.

7.

8.

9. **EverLink**™

10.

11.

12.

13.

14.

15.

1		
Design Firm	**Wynn Art Direction**	
2, 9		
Design Firm	**Squires & Company**	
3, 12		
Design Firm	**Smart Design Inc.**	
4		
Design Firms	**J.J. Sedelmaier Productions, Inc., Yoe! Studio**	
5, 7, 11, 14, 15		
Design Firm	**Pedersen Gesk**	
6		
Design Firm	**ID8 (RTKL Associates Inc.)**	
8, 13		
Design Firm	**Mires Design, Inc.**	
10		
Design Firm	**Conflux Design**	

1.		
Client	*VLSI Technology, Inc.*	
Designer	Christopher Wynn	
2.		
Client	*Deep Ellum Association*	
Designer	Paul Black	
3.		
Client	*Berlex*	
Designers	Tom Dair, Tam Thomsen, Evelyn Teploff	
4.		
Client	*MTV Networks/Nickelodeon*	
Designers	J.J. Sedelmaier, Craig Yoe	
5.		
Client	*Schwan's Sales Ent.*	
Designer	Rony Zibara	

6.		
Client	*Turnberry Associates*	
Designer	Charlie Greenawalt	
7.		
Client	*Grand Metropolitan*	
8.		
Client	*Nike, Inc.*	
Designers	John Ball, Miguel Perez	
9.		
Client	*Anyware Technologies*	
Creative Director		
	Paul Black	
Designer	Anna Magruder	
10.		
Client	*Digital Textures*	
Designer	Greg Fedorev	
11.		
Client	*Pepsi-Co Company*	
Designer	Rony Zibara, Pepsi-Co	
12.		
Client	*OXO International*	
Designers	Davin Stowell, Rie Norregaard	
13.		
Client	*Nike Inc.*	
Designers	Scott Mires, Mike Brower	
14.		
Client	*The Clorox Company*	
Designers	Rony Zibara, Morgan Brig, Julie So	
15.		
Client	*Jim Beam Brands*	
Designers	Rony Zibara, Andrea Williams	

IMPERIAL BANCORP

1.

Merry Mary Fabrics, Inc.

2.

THE
KEYSTONE
SOCIETY

3.

WOMEN'S
HEALTH
CONNECTION

4.

BONNEVILLE PRODUCTIONS

5.

KAWabunga!

6.

7.

1, 2, 5-7
Design Firm **Yuguchi Group, Inc.**
3, 4
Design Firm **Emphasis Seven Communications, Inc.**

1.
Client   *Imperial Bank*
Designer Clifford Yuguchi
2.
Client   *Merry Mary Fabric*
Designer Clifford Yuguchi
3.
Client   *Resurrection Health Care (The Keystone Society)*
Designers E7ci Staff Designers
4.
Client   *Resurrection Health Care (Women's Health Connection)*
Designer Debra Nemeth

5.
Client   *Bonneville Productions*
Designer Clifford Yuguchi
6.
Client   *Kawasaki*
Designer Clifford Yuguchi
7.
Client   *Pizza Hut*
Designer Clifford Yuguchi
(opposite)
Client   *Monrovia*
Design Firm **Maureen Erbe Design**
Designers Maureen Erbe, Efi Latief, Rita Sowins

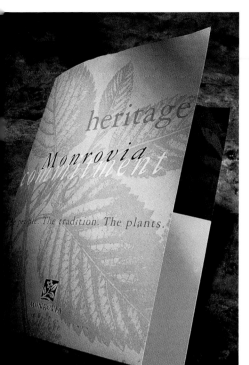

1.

Advantage**kbs**

2.

The Linus Pauling Institute

3.

4.

*corporate**computing** e x p o*

5.

OpenCon Systems, Inc.

WORLDWIDE COMMUNICATIONS SOLUTIONS

6.

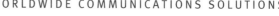

7.

CHRISTINA FIELDS
CIBTAC. A.o.R. Pract. Assoc. MAR.
Clinical Reflexolgist

8.

Pasadena Civic Ballet

9.

10.

11.

12.

13.

14.

15.

1, 4, 7, 10, 11, 14, 15
   Design Firm **Zunda Design Group**
2, 5, 6, 12, 13
   Design Firm **David Morris Creative, Inc.**
3, 8, 9
   Design Firm **Corporate Visuals**
1.
   Client   *Hershey Chocolate U.S.A.*
   Designer Charles Zunda
2.
   Client   *Advantagekbs*
   Designer Glenn Gontha
3.
   Client   *Linus Pauling Institute*
   Designer Ronald Rampley
4.
   Client   *Zunda Design Group*
   Designers Charles Zunda, Jon Voss
5.
   Client   *JKW*
   Designer Glenn Gontha
6.
   Client   *OpenCon Systems, Inc.*
   Designer Matt Gilbert

7.
   Client   *Best Foods Baking*
   Designer Charles Zunda
8.
   Designer Ronald Rampley
9.
   Client   *Pasadena Civic Ballet*
   Designer Ronald Rampley
10.
   Client   *Personal Care Group*
   Designers Charles Zunda, Greg Martin
11.
   Client   *Ben & Jerry's Homemade, Inc.*
   Designer Charles Zunda
12.
   Client   *Firewheel Automotive*
   Designer Tim O'Donnell
13.
   Client   *DMS*
   Designer Matt Gilbert
14.
   Client   *Hershey Chocolate U.S.A.*
   Designer Charles Zunda
15.
   Client   *Hershey Chocolate U.S.A.*
   Designers Charles Zunda, Maija Riekstins

1.

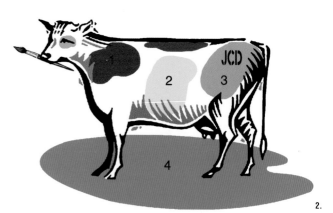

2.

3.

4.

SONRISA
RANCHO · DEL · REY

5.

Tautron

6.

RANCHO DOS CAÑADAS

7.

1.

custom
SOLUTIONS
From A Texas Utilities Company™

2.

3.

4.

MONY

5.

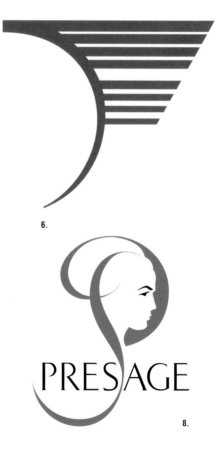

6.

PRESAGE

8.

7.

230

9.

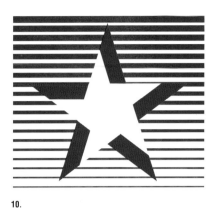

10.

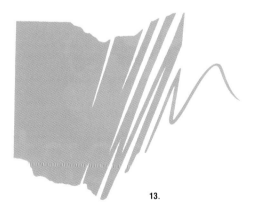

11.

15.

12.

13.

14.

1, 10, 12
Design Firm **Coleman Design Group, Inc.**

2, 4, 9, 11
Design Firm **Griffith Phillips Creative**
Creative Director
Ken Phillips

3, 5, 7, 13, 14
Design Firm **Waters Design Associates Inc.**
Creative Director
John Waters

6, 8, 15
Design Firm **John Stribiak & Assoc.**

1.
Client — Manor Style
Designer — John Coleman

2.
Client — Texas Utilities Electric Company
Designer — Brian Niemann

3.
Client — Military Benefit Association
Designer — Linda Grimm

4.
Client — Sprint
Creative Director
Ken Phillips
Designer — Brian Niemann

5.
Client — The Mutual Life Insurance Company of New York
Designer — Clint Morgan

6.
Client — Design Facets
Designer — John Stribiak

7.
Client — Young Presidents Organization
Designer — Bob Kellerman

8.
Client — Presage
Designer — John Stribiak

9.
Client — GTE
Designer — Tony Stubbs

10.
Client — United Technologies
Designers — John Coleman, Eric Goetz

11.
Client — GTE
Designer — Tony Stubbs

12.
Client — Coleman Design Group, Inc.
Designer — John Coleman

13.
Client — Ohio Arts Council
Designer — Bob Kellerman

14.
Client — Arrow Electronics, Inc.
Designer — Linda Grimm

15.
Client — Associated Design Services
Designer — John Stribiak

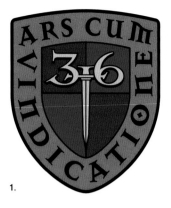

1.

3.

REMEDIATION RESOURCES, INC.

4.

6.

7.

RAPAX

8.

234

Page *One*

Business Productions, L.L.C.

9.

10.

ShokT

11.

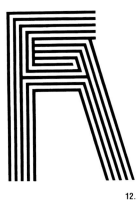

12.

13.

14.

15.

1, 4, 8, 9, 11, 14
Design Firm **30sixty design, Inc.**
2, 3, 5-7, 10, 12, 13, 15
Design Firm **Sommese Design**

1.
Client — *30sixty design, Inc.*
Designers — Pär Larsson, Henry Vizcarra

2.
Client — *Dantes Restaurants Inc.*
Designer — Lanny Sommese

3.
Client — *Ralph Licastro C.P.A.*
Designer — Lanny Sommese

4.
Client — *Remediation Resources, Inc.*
Designer — Pär Larsson

5.
Client — *Aquatics & Exotics*
Designer — Lanny Sommese

6.
Client — *Penn State Summer Fest Theatre*
Designer — Lanny Sommese

7.
Client — *Dante's Restaurants Inc.*
Designer — Lanny Sommese

8.
Client — *RAPAX*
Designer — Henry Vizcarra

9.
Client — *Page One Business Productions, L.L.C.*
Designer — Pär Larsson

10.
Client — *Remodelers Workshop*
Designers — Lanny Sommese, Kristin Sommese

11.
Client — *Shokt*
Designer — Rickard Olsson

12.
Client — *Fitness America*
Designer — Lanny Sommese

13.
Client — *Hoag's Catering*
Designer — Lanny Sommese

14.
Client — *30sixty design, Inc.*
Designer — Pär Larsson

15.
Client — *Women's Awareness Group, Penn State University*
Designer — Kristin Sommese

1.

2.

SCOTT STOLL

PHOTOGRAPHY

3.

The Park

4.

IW LAHTI DESIGN, WEST

5.

SUNDOWN

SAFARI

6.

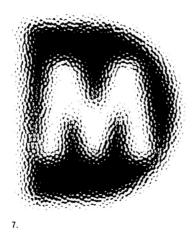

7.

FUTURE

FORUM

8.

9.

10.

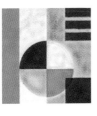

BELYEA DESIGN ALLIANCE

11.

GLOBAL CAPITAL SECURITIES, INC.

12.

13.

 Salty Dog Productions, Inc.

14.

15.

1.

i !
impact
2. U N L I M I T E D

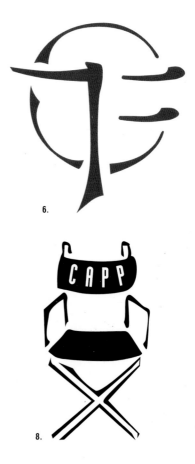

THE Jewish Center FOR
Community Services
3. OF EASTERN FAIRFIELD COUNTY

THE EDUCATORS NETWORK®
4. Linking Consultants and Trainers with Industry and Government

5.

6.

ISP·TV
7.

CAPP
8.

THE SN⌓RING
INSTITUTE ★
9.

10.

WOLFROM HOMES
11.

HERITAGE GREEN
AT HOBBIT'S GLEN
12.

13.

Search**Alliance**
14.

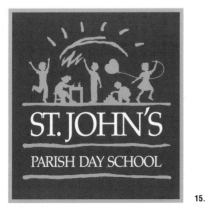
15.

AmericanAirlines

1.

2.

SKY CHEFS

3.

4.

PRATT &
WHITNEY

5.

Raritan

6.

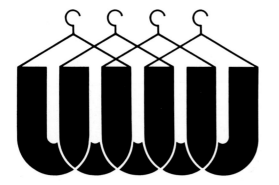

7.

1-3, 5, 6
Design Firm **Henry Dreyfuss Associates**
4
Design Firm **Capt Flynn Advertising**
7
Design Firm **Tri-Arts Studio**
1.
Client *American Airlines*
2.
Client *Bankers Trust*
3.
Client *Sky Chefs*
4.
Client *International Institute for Literacy*
Designer Tom Rigsby

5.
Client *Pratt & Whitney*
6.
Client *Raritan*
7.
Client *Uniforms Unlimited*
Designer Tom Rigsby
Artist Richard Vartian
(opposite)
Client *Deere & Company*
Design Firm **Henry Dreyfuss Associates**

1.

2.

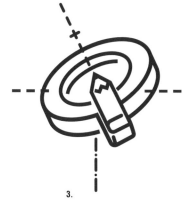

3.

4.

5.

6.

CHICAGO

7.

8.

9.

10.

11.

12.

13.

14. LOS ANGELES

15.

(all)
Design Firm **Mike Quon/Designation Inc.**
Designer **Mike Quon**

1.
Client *American Express*
2.
Client *Dream Makers/Japan*
3.
Client *Mike Quon Design Office*
4.
Client *American Express*
5.
Client *American Express*
6.
Client *British Airways*
7.
Client *British Airways*

8.
Client *Bell Atlantic*
9.
Client *Intergold*
10.
Client *Philip Morris*
11.
Client *American Express*
12.
Client *American Express*
13.
Client *Center for Public Resources*
14.
Client *British Airways*
15.
Client *Good Times Home Video*

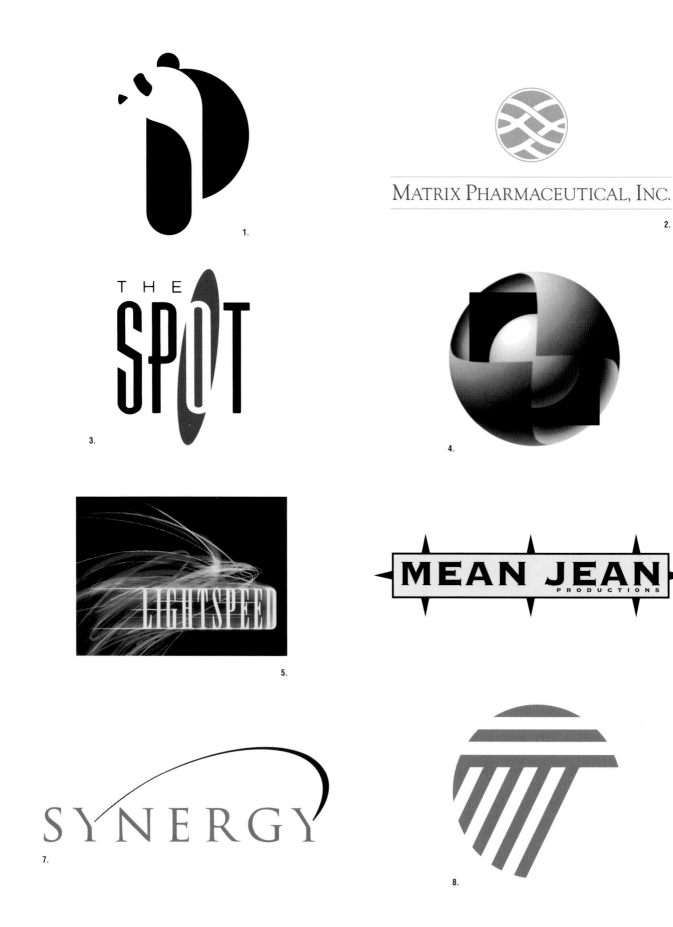

MATRIX PHARMACEUTICAL, INC.

1.

2.

THE
SPOT

3.

4.

LIGHTSPEED

5.

MEAN JEAN
PRODUCTIONS

6.

SYNERGY

7.

8.

ARTEMIS®

9.

10.

11.

12.

13.

SINO(GEN

14.

15.

1.

Investment Horizons

2.

3.

Perfect Sense

P R O D U C T S

4.

5.

6.

7.

8.

246

HEALTHY UTAH

The Art of Fitness

9.

10.

OWL RIDGE
VINEYARD

11.

12.

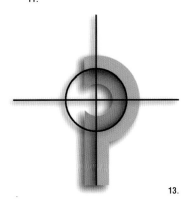

13.

14.

15.

1.

2.

THE

at eagle mountain

PARK MEADOWS

3.

PEHP

WeeCare

4.

5.

6.

OASIS

ACADEMY

7.

8.

NUTRACEUTICAL

248

9.

10.

11.

MICRO BREW

12.

B

BONNEVILLE
M A C H I N E

13.

14.

NETWORK™
MULTIMEDIA

15.

(all)
Design Firm **Richard & Swensen, Inc.**

1.
Client   *Utah Symphony*
Designer William Swensen

2.
Client   *Dunn Communications*
Designer Louis Johnson

3.
Client   *Public Employees Health Program*
Designer William Swensen

4.
Client   *Salt Lake Acting Co.*
Designers Micheal Richards, William Swensen

5.
Client   *I.N.V.U.*
Designer Micheal Richards

6.
Client   *Oasis Academy*
Designer Micheal Richards

7.
Client   *KUED Channel 7*
Designers Micheal Richards, Alan Loyborg

8.
Client   *Dunn Communications*
Designer William Swensen

9.
Client   *University of Utah*
Designers Micheal Richards, William Swensen

10.
Client   *U.S. Figure Skating Assoc.*
Designers Micheal Richards, William Swensen

11.
Client   *U.S. Figure Skating Assoc.*
Designers Micheal Richards, William Swensen

12.
Client   *Network Multimedia*
Designer William Swensen

13.
Client   *Bonneville Machine*
Designers Micheal Richards,
          Connie Christensen

14.
Client   *Redman Moving & Storage*
Designer Michael Richards

15.
Client   *Network Multimedia*
Designers William Swensen, Michael Low

1.

2.

3.

4.

GAC
GRAPHIC ARTS CENTER

5.

6.

7.

8.

250

9.

10.

celestial

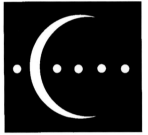

harmonies

11.

12.

13.

COTTONWOOD PROPERTIES

14.

15.

1-4, 6-15		
Design Firm	**Boelts Bros. Associates**	
Designers	Eric Boelts, Jackson Boelts, Kerry Stratford	
5		
Design Firm	**The DuPuis Group**	

1.
Client	Acid Rain

2.
Client	Peccary King Productions

3.
Client	Southwest School of Music

4.
Client	Tucson Art Expo

5.
Client	GAC (Graphic Art Center)
Designer	Hasyun Ruettgers

6.
Client	Southwest Traditions

7.
Client	Men's 20/30 Club of Tucson

8.
Client	Ringo Starr/Sierra Tucson Foundation

9.
Client	Epic Café

10.
Client	University of Arizona

11.
Client	Celestial Harmonies

12.
Client	River Road Brewery

13.
Client	Estabon Apodaca

14.
Client	Cottonwood Properties

15.
Client	Men's 20/30 Club of Tucson

KEYTECH
ASSOCIATES

1.

RiverViewGolf

2.

theKEYS

3.

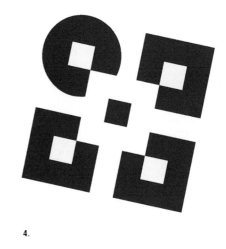

4.

SOUND
ADVICE

5.

PHARMACEUTICAL TECHNOLOGIES, INC.

6.

7.

DAYSPRING

8.

9.

10.

Wharton

11.

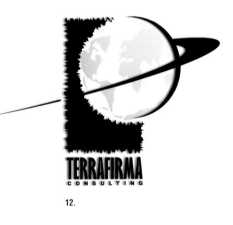

TERRAFIRMA
CONSULTING

12.

the creative center

13.

14.

15.

CAPRI
HEART & LUNG INSTITUTE

1.

HARRISON

2.

3.

ECLIPSE

4.

KINGS HILL

5.

GRACIE'S

6.

7.

1-3, 6
Design Firm **Snodgrass Design Associates**
4, 5
Design Firm **John Langdon Design**
7
Design Firm **TLG**
1.
Client   *Capri-Heart & Lung Institute*
Designer Leslie Snodgrass
2.
Client   *Harrison Hospital*
Designer Leslie Snodgrass
3.
Client   *St. Helens Sparkling Mountain Water*
Designer Leslie Snodgrass

4.
Client   *Oberheim*
Designer John Langdon
5.
Client   *Willard Rouse Developers*
Designer John Langdon
6.
Client   *Gracie's Restaurant*
Designer Leslie Snodgrass
7.
Client   *Vernell's Candy Company*
Designer Leslie Snodgrass
(opposite)
Client   *Gais Bakery*
Design Firm **TLG**
Designer Leslie Snodgrass

1.

2.

3.

4. HAWKINS CONSTRUCTION COMPANY

5. Bill Drake MUSIC

6.

7. fX SPORTS

8. TANNENBAUM'S OLD MARKET FLORIST

9.

10.

11.

12.

13.

CONDOLINK

14.

15.

1.

Oridion

2.

3.

4.

beans

NetScout

5.

6.

7.

Northern Light

8.

parky

The Park School Wonder Dog

9.

10.

Queen *of* CLEAN

11.

Coffee

12.

13.

LUCY'S LACES

14.

A B A C O

15.

(all)
Design Firm **Gill Fishman Associates, Inc.**

1.
Client *Oridion Medical*
Designer Michael Persons

2.
Client *Standard Uniform*
Designers Fred Odlinko, Gill Fishman

3.
Client *Symbiotics*
Designers Condee Freeman, Gill Fishman

4.
Client *Beans Coffees*
Designers Gill Fishman, Anne Alvarez

5.
Client *Netscout Software*
Designers Alicia Ozyjowski, Gill Fishman

6.
Client *Editions Judaica*
Designer Gill Fishman

7.
Client *Northern Light*
Designers Michael Persons, Alicia Ozyjowski, Gill Fishman

8.
Client *The Park School*
Designer Gill Fishman

9.
Client *Digital Delivery*
Designer Michael Persons

10.
Client *Inso Corp.*
Designers Gill Fishman, Condee Freeman

11.
Client *Queen of Clean*
Designers Nora Higgins, Gill Fishman

12.
Client *Haagen Dazs*
Designers Michael Persons, Gill Fishman

13.
Client *Rainboworld*
Designer Gill Fishman

14.
Client *Lucy's Laces*
Designers Gill Fishman, Ann Casady

15.
Client *Abaco*
Designer Michael Persons

I M A G E R Y
S O F T W A R E

1.

Kurzweil
Educational
Systems

2.

3.

VIS

4.

PACIFIC
OCEAN
GROUP
I N C.

5.

6.

BIG GREEN

7.

DEL ORO
REGIONAL RESOUCE CENTER

8.

ROMANOW

CONTAINER

9.

TM

UNITED STATES
POSTAL SERVICE

OFFICIAL OLYMPIC SPONSOR

10.

11.

DANNON®

12.

13.

Eastern Casualty

14.

15.

1.

2.

RANDALL
MUSEUM

3.

4.

BAUER

5.

WHITE OAK

NIMAN

RANCH

6.

7.

8.

264

9.

10.

11.

12.

planet U

13.

computers**America**™

14.

15.

1, 4, 5, 7, 9, 15
Design Firm **Pinkhaus Design**
2
Design Firm **Joe Advertising**
3, 6, 8, 10-14
Design Firm **CookSherman**

1.
Client   *Mercury Restaurant*
Designer Todd Houser
2.
Client   *Kelly's Coffee*
Designer Sharon Occhipinti
3.
Client   *Randall Museum Friends*
Designers Ken Cook, Inica Mucia
4.
Client   *Café Cofé Restaurant*
Designers Todd Houser, Joel Fuller
5.
Client   *Nike—Bauer In-Line Skates*
Designer John Norman
6.
Client   *Boisseau Evans & Associates*
          White Oak
Designer C. Randall Sherman

7.
Client   *Garment Corporation of America*
Designers Joel Fuller, Laura Latham
8.
Client   *Niman Ranch*
Designer Ken Cook
9.
Client   *Daniel Williams, Architect*
Designer Joel Fuller
10.
Client   *Digital Imaging Group*
Designers Ken Cook, I-Hua Chen
11.
Client   *Calyx & Corolla Flower*
Designer Ken Cook
12.
Client   *Andromedia*
Designers Ken Cook, Louisa Louie
13.
Client   *Planet U*
Designers Ken Cook, I-Hua Chen
14.
Client   *Kallen Computer Products*
Designers Ken Cook, I-Hua Chen
15.
Client   *Pepsi Stuff*
Designers John Norman, Mark Cantor,
          Todd Houser

1.

2.

3.

GENES|S

4.

VA(U)LT™

5.

6.

7.

1-3, 6, 7
Design Firm **Hornall Anderson Design Works**
4, 5
Design Firm **Internal Creative Department, CheckFree Corporation**

1.
Client *The Summit at Snoqualmie*
Designers Jack Anderson, David Bates, Sonja Max

2.
Client *XactData Corporation*
Designers Jack Anderson, Lisa Cerveny, Jana Wilson, Julie Keenan

3.
Client *Bruce Clark Productions*
Designers Jack Anderson, Heidi Favour, Mary Hermes

4.
Client *CheckFree Corporation*
Designer Michael Higgins

5.
Client *CheckFree Corporation*
Designer Michael Higgins

6.
Client *Food Services of America*
Designers Jack Anderson, Cliff Chung, Scott Eggers, Leo Raymundo, Bruce Branson-Meyer

7.
Client *Food Services of America*
Designer Jack Anderson
(opposite)
Client *CW Gourmet/Mondeo*
Design Firm **Hornall Anderson Design Works**
Designers Jack Anderson, David Bates, Sonja Max

mondéo

1.

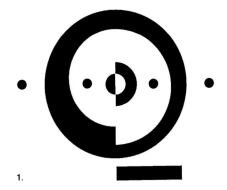

2.

Digital Island®
www.digisle.net

3.

4.

JIM **SPORTS** KELLY

6.

5.

7.

1, 4, 5
Design Firm **Hornall Anderson Design Works**
2, 6, 7
Design Firm **Gold & Associates**
3
Design Firm **Max Graphics**
1.
Client *Quebecor Integrated Media*
Designers Jack Anderson, Heidi Favour,
Mary Hermes, Mary Chin
Hutchinson, Julia LaPine
2.
Client *Harcourt Brace*
Designers Keith Gold, Joseph Vavra
3.
Client *Digital Island*
Designers Bob Schonfisch, Ron Higgins

4.
Client *Jamba Juice*
Designers Jack Anderson, Lisa Cerveny,
Suzanne Haddon
5.
Client *Hornall Anderson Design Works*
Designers Jack Anderson, David Bates
6.
Client *Jim Kelly*
Designers Keith Gold, Raul Febles
7.
Client *Time Life Music*
Designers Keith Gold, Joseph Vavra
(opposite)
Client *Best Cellars*
Design Firm **Hornall Anderson Design Works**
Designers Jack Anderson, Lisa Cerveny,
Jana Wilson

271

VerSecure

1.

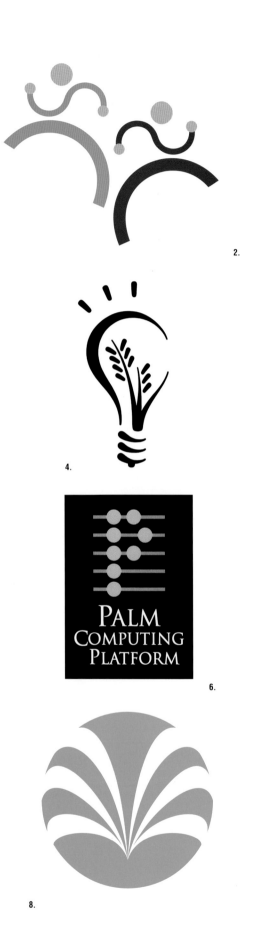

2.

3.

4.

radius

5.

**PALM
COMPUTING
PLATFORM**

6.

ALASKAN · PURE · NATURAL · HARVEST · SEAFOOD ·

7.

8.

Lily's Alterations

9.

SOUTH UMPQUA
B · A · N · K

10.

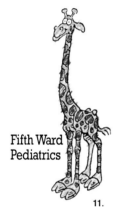

Fifth Ward
Pediatrics

11.

r e n d i t i o n

12.

C-CUBE

13.

The Children's Doctors

14.

kor

15.

1, 5, 6, 10, 12, 13
 Design Firm **Mortensen Design**
2, 3, 8, 15
 Design Firm **Kor Group**
4
 Design Firm **Hornall Anderson Design Works**
7
 Design Firm **Faine/Oller Productions**
9, 11, 14
 Design Firm **Ramsden Design**

1.
 Client — *Hewlett Packard*
 Designers — Diana L. Kauzlarich,
 Gordon Mortensen

2.
 Client — *Giant Steps*
 Designer — M.B. Sawyer

3.
 Client — *Potts Design*
 Designers — Karen Dendy, Kor Group,
 Amy Potts, Potts Design

4.
 Client — *Food Services of America*
 Designers — Jack Anderson, Cliff Chung,
 Heidi Favour, Debra McCloskey,
 Julie Lock

5.
 Client — *Radius*
 Designer — Gordon Mortensen

6.
 Designers — Gordon Mortensen, Wendy Chon

7.
 Client — *Alaskan Harvest Seafoods*
 Designers — Catherine Oller, Barbara Faine,
 Jerry Nelson

8.
 Client — *Stone Center/*
 Wellesley Centers for Women
 Designer — Karen Dendy

9.
 Client — *Lily's Alterations*
 Designer — Rosalie Ramsden

10.
 Client — *South Umpqua Bank*
 Designer — Gordon Mortensen

11.
 Client — *Fifth Ward Pediatrics*
 Designer — Rosalie Ramsden

12.
 Client — *Rendition*
 Designer — Gordon Mortensen
 Illustrator — John Bleck

13.
 Client — *C-Cube Microsystems*
 Designer — Gordon Mortensen

14.
 Client — *The Children's Doctors*
 Designer — Rosalie Ramsden

15.
 Client — *Kor Group*
 Designers — Karen Dendy, Anne Callahan,
 M.B. Sawyer

1.

2.

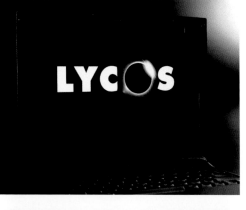

3.

4.

5.

6.

(all)
Design Firm **Wallace Church Assoc., Inc.**
1.
  Client   *Bayer*
  Designers   Stan Church, Derek Samuel
2.
  Client   *Ultrafem Inc.*
  Designers   Stan Church, Wendy Church,
               Derek Samuel
3.
  Client   *Lycos*
  Designers   Stan Church, Craig Swanson
4.
  Client   *Spalding Sports Worldwide*
  Designers   Stan Church, John Waski,
               David Ceradini

5.
  Client   *Frito Lay*
  Designers   Stan Church, Phyllis Chan-Carr
6.
  Client   *Smith Kline Beecham*
  Designers   Stan Church, Phyllis Chan-Carr
(opposite)
  Client   *Dunlop Maxfli Sports Corp.*
  Design Firm **Wallace Church Assoc., Inc.**
  Designers   Stan Church, Bob Russell, John
               Waski, Derek Samuel

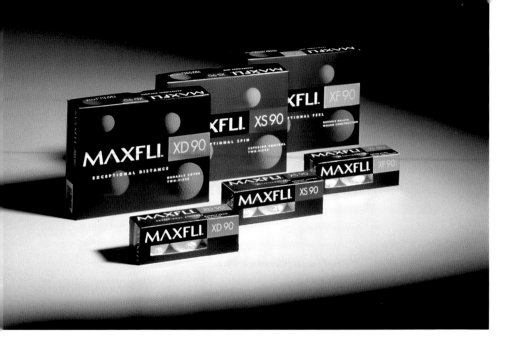

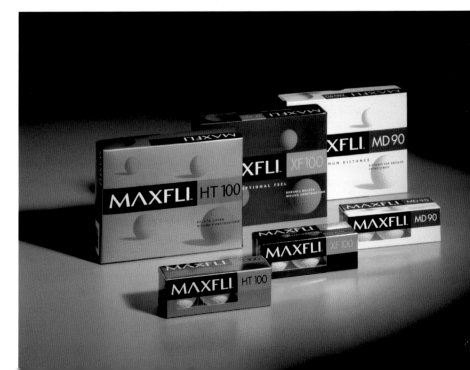

1.

GUTHY·RENKER™

2.

3.

Surgery Centers
of the Desert

4.

HOTH FINE *& Company*
THE HOME BUYER'S CONSULTANT

5.

Our Savior's Community

6.

Chaney
ENTERPRISES

7.

THE DIAMOND COLLECTION
The Final Phase at Morningside

8.

ConDel corp

9.

PETTIT
CONSTRUCTION, LLC ™

10.

BUILDING BRIDGES & BEYOND
SOUTHWEST COMMUNITY CHURCH

11.

STARTER

12.

The Westin Mission Hills

13.

MASTER POOLS ™

14.

DESIGN
DEVELOPMENT ■
Innovative Architecture

15.

279

1. ATHERTON

2. synergy

3. TURNSTONE

4.

5. B A L B O A

6.

7. D A N C I N G D E S E R T P R E S S

8.

 **ViroLogic**

9.

10.

11.

 EMPART

12.

 INTER**A**CTIVE

14.

13.

15.

281

1.

2.

3.

4.

5.

6.

7.

8.

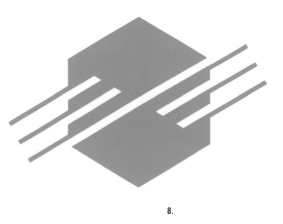

9.

10.

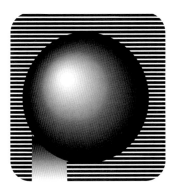

11.

Biocycle

12.

13.

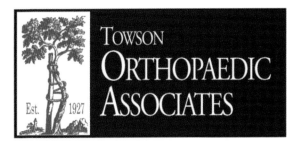

14.

ARISTA
Advertising & Design

15.

**PRECISION
COLOR**
Innovative Imaging

1.

2.

3.

4.

DIVERSITY

5.

6.

ECLIPSE

7.

284

Mild and Natural™

285

MOUNTAIN TOP
Heavy Equipment Repair & Service, Inc.

1.

CARMEL MARINA CORPORATION

2.

3.

4.

5.

6.

7.

8.

NAVℓCOM

9.

AQUARESEARCH

10.

BOWTIE BILLIARDS

11.

FallingSun
PUBLICATIONS

12.

McABEE BEACH Cafe

13.

14.

JAMES GOODE

CONSTRUCTION

15.

1-3, 5-13		
Design Firm	**The Wecker Group**	
4, 14, 15		
Design Firm	**Horvath Design**	
1.		
Client	*Mountain Top Repair*	
Designer	Robert J. Wecker	
2.		
Client	*Carmel Marina Corporation*	
Designer	Robert J. Wecker	
3.		
Client	*Sunset Tennis Classic*	
Designer	Robert J. Wecker	
4.		
Client	*Dr. Art Weisman*	
Designer	Kevin Horvath	
5.		
Client	*The Racer's Group*	
Designers	Robert J. Wecker, Matt Gnibus	
6.		
Client	*Blue Fin Billiards*	
Designer	Robert J. Wecker	

7.	
Client	*Universal Internet*
Designer	Robert J. Wecker
8.	
Client	*Morgan Winery*
Designer	Robert J. Wecker
9.	
Client	*Navecom*
Designer	Robert J. Wecker
10.	
Client	*Aquafuture*
Designer	Robert J. Wecker
11.	
Client	*Bow Tie Billiards*
Designers	Robert J. Wecker, Matt Gnibus
12.	
Client	*Falling Sun Publications*
Designer	Robert J. Wecker
13.	
Client	*McAbee Beach Cafe*
Designers	Robert J. Wecker, James Kyllo
14.	
Client	*Investment Securities*
Designer	Kevin Horvath
15.	
Client	*James Goode Construction*
Designer	Kevin Horvath

1895   1995
GLEN RIDGE
CENTENNIAL

1.

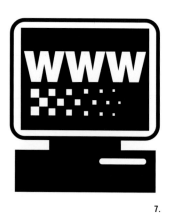

2.

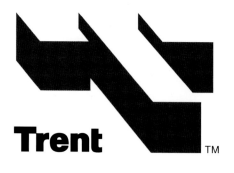

Trent™

3.

LiFE™
INSTRUCTORS INC

4.

5.

6.

7.

8.

288

9.

CARDIAC
EMERGENCY
NETWORK

10.

11.

12.

Bellin Heartwatch Plus:
New Ideas
for Healthy Living

13.

WOMEN'S
HEALTH CENTER
AT CLARA MAASS

14.

Bellin Hospital

15.

1-9, 11, 14
   Design Firm **The Design Shop**
10, 13, 15
   Design Firm **Bellin Hospital Marketing/**
               Communications Dept.
12
   Design Firm **Dan Meehan Design**
1.
   Client   *Glen Ridge Historical Society*
   Designer Bill Wood
2.
   Client   *Glen Ridge Congregational Church*
   Designer Bill Wood
3.
   Client   *Trent Corporation*
   Designer Bill Wood
4.
   Client   *Life Instructors Inc.*
   Designer Bill Wood
5.
   Client   *Bell Atlantic*
   Designer Bill Wood
6.
   Client   *Borough of Glen Ridge NJ*
   Designer Bill Wood

7.
   Client   *National Exchange Carrier Assoc.*
   Designer Bill Wood
8.
   Client   *Sigma Software Inc.*
   Designer Bill Wood
9.
   Client   *Rockland Corporation*
   Designer Bill Wood
10.
   Client   *Bellin Hospital/Cardiac*
               Emergency Network
   Designer Daniel Green
11.
   Client   *Computer Power Inc.*
   Designer Bill Wood
12.
   Client   *Precision Mowing & Lawn*
               Maintenance
   Designer Dan Meehan
13.
   Client   *Bellin Heartwatch Plus*
   Designer Daniel Green
14.
   Client   *Clara Maass Medical Center*
   Designer Bill Wood
15.
   Client   *Bellin Hospital*
   Designer Daniel Green

1.

2.

3.

4.

5.

6.

7.

8.

9.

10.

11.

12.

13.

COLORADO MASSAGE

C E N T E R

14.

GEODE

15.

(all)
Design Firm **Robert W. Taylor Design, Inc.**

1.
Client — *Boulder Philharmonic Orchestra*
Designer — Clyde Mason

2.
Client — *Colorado Christian Home*
Designer — Robert W. Taylor

3.
Client — *Symbion, Inc.*
Designer — Laura Schnell

4.
Client — *Colorado Special Olympics*
Designers — Robert W. Taylor, David Schenk, René Bobo

5.
Client — *ERIC Group, Inc.*
Designers — Robert W. Taylor, Kathleen Stier, Anne Deister

6.
Client — *Aeronautics Leasing, Inc.*
Designer — Robert W. Taylor, Karey Christ-Janer

7.
Client — *Rocky Mountain Translators*
Designer — Anne Deister

8.
Client — *Vail Valley Foundation*
Designer — Anne Deister

9.
Client — *Longmont Foods Company, Inc.*
Designers — Robert W. Taylor, Tim Stortz

10.
Client — *The Community Foundation Serving Boulder County*
Designers — Robert W. Taylor, Susan Davis

11.
Client — *Monfort of Colorado, Inc.*
Designer — Chuck Arndt

12.
Client — *City and County of Denver*
Designers — Robert W. Taylor, Clyde Mason, Kathleen Stier

13.
Client — *Vail Valley Foundation*
Designer — Kathleen Stier

14.
Client — *Colorado Massage Center*
Designer — Neil Quiddington

15.
Client — *Geode Consulting, LLC*
Designers — Robert W. Taylor, Lorisa Neff, Alan Hesker

1.

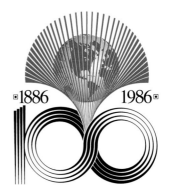

2.

3.

4.

5.

6.

peconic ELECTRONIC

7.

8.

9.

10.

omni
OFFICE SYSTEMS

11.

TAPAWINGO
NATIONAL GOLF CLUB

12.

13.

14.

15.

1-3, 6, 9, 12, 13
Design Firm **The Weber Group Inc.**
4, 7, 8, 10, 11
Design Firm **Callery & Company**
14
Design Firm **Summit Advertising**
15
Design Firm **Madison Avenue East**
1.
  Client   *J.C. Pendergast*
  Designer Jeff Tischer
2.
  Client   *S.C. Johnson & Son, Inc.*
  Designer Anthony Weber
3.
  Client   *Access Outreach Services*
  Designer Anthony Weber
4.
  Client   *LI Philharmonic*
  Designer Kelley Callery
5.
  Client   *FFTA (Flexsys)*
  Designer Kelley Callery

6.
  Client   *The Docks*
  Designer Anthony Weber
7.
  Client   *Peconic Electronic*
  Designer Kelley Callery
8.
  Client   *LN Marketing*
  Designer Kelley Callery
9.
  Client   *S.C. Johnson & Son, Inc.*
  Designer Anthony Weber
10.
  Client   *NJ Cougars*
  Designer Kelley Callery
11.
  Client   *Omni Office Systems*
  Designer Kelley Callery
12.
  Client   *Tapawingo National Golf Club*
  Designer Anthony Weber
13.
  Client   *S.C. Johnson & Son, Inc.*
  Designer Anthony Weber
14.
  Client   *Summit Advertising*
  Designer Kelley Callery
15.
  Client   *North Fork Bank*
  Designer Kelley Callery

1.

COZY COUNTRYSIDE COUNSELING

2.

RǪEHM
Renovation Contractor

3.

E-B

4.

SIMANTEL | GROUP

5.

Tuneshare

6.

HANSON
CLEANERS

7.

8.

296

On-Line

MAD COW FARMS

9.

10.

Truckin' Time

ONCLAVE™

12.

11.

INSTANT HEALTHLINE

14.

13.

AFTER THE
FLOOD

15.

1-7, 9-15
Design Firm **Simantel Group**

8
Design Firm **The Weber Group Inc.**

1.
Client *Jim's Gym*
Designer Wendy Behrens

2.
Client *Debbie Krause*
Designer Wendy Behrens

3.
Client *Roehm Renovations*
Designer Becky Krohe

4.
Client *Eric Behrens - Photojournalist*
Designer Wendy Behrens

5.
Client *Simantel Group*
Designer Chris Moehn

6.
Client *Tuneshare*
Designer Becky Krohe

7.
Client *Hanson Cleaners*
Designer Wendy Behrens

8.
Client *S.C. Johnson & Sons, Inc.*
Designer Anthony Weber

9.
Client *CEFCU*
Designer Wendy Behrens

10.
Client *Mad Cow Farms*
Designer Lisa Lucas

11.
Client *Caterpillar Inc.*
Designer Wendy Behrens

12.
Client *Internet Dynamics, Inc.*
Designer Lisa Lucas

13.
Client *Mitsubishi Motors LPGA Charity Pro-Am*
Designer Molly Vonachen

14.
Client *SVI Inc.*
Designer Chris Moehn

15.
Client *Peoria Journal Star*
Designer Wendy Behrens

1.

2.

3.

4.

5.

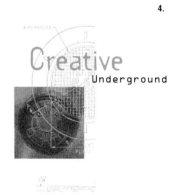

6.

7.

8.

9.

10.

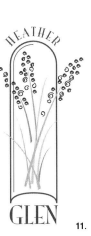

11.

12.

13.

CR☉SSR☉ADS

14.

15.

299

Kalpana

1.

2.

Datascope

3.

DANIELA VEO

4.

Beach House

5.

LUCILE SALTER PACKARD
CHILDREN'S HOSPITAL AT STANFORD

6.

REFLECT 15
SUNSCREEN

7.

8.

300

SummaCare

9.

 Compact Devices

10.

PhoenixNetwork.

11.

 **Calypso** SM
IMAGING

12.

GENESYS

13.

JOGA CHIROPRACTIC CENTER

14.

 salusmedia

15.

 B.E.S.T.
PROGRAM

BREAST EXAMINATION
SELF-TEACHING

16.

1, 10, 13
Design Firm **Howry Design Associates**
2, 6
Design Firm **S & O Consultants**
3-5, 7, 9, 11, 12, 15
Design Firm **AERIAL**
8, 14
Design Firm **Kristin Odermatt Design**
16
Design Firm **Diane Kuntz Design**

1.
  Client   *Kalpana*
  Designer & Art Director
     Jill Howry
2.
  Client   *PG&E*
  Designers Tracy Moon, Tony Hyun
3.
  Client   *Datascope Corp.*
  Designer Tracy Moon
4.
  Client   *DFS Group Limited*
  Designer Tracy Moon
5.
  Client   *Pacific Beach House, Inc.*
  Designer Tracy Moon
6.
  Client   *Lucile Salter Packard Children's Hospital at Stanford*
  Designer Tracy Moon

7.
  Client   *Reflect Inc.*
  Designer Tracy Moon
8.
  Client   *Veneklasen Associates*
  Designers Kristin Odermatt, Deanna McClure
9.
  Client   *Summa Care/Collagen Corp.*
  Designer Tracy Moon
10.
  Client   *Compact Devices*
  Art Director Jill Howry
  Designer Craig Forsdick
11.
  Client   *Phoenix Network*
  Designer Tracy Moon
12.
  Client   *Calypso Imaging*
  Designer Tracy Moon
13.
  Client   *Genesys*
  Art Director Jill Howry
  Designer Michael Mescall
14.
  Client   *Joga Chiropractic Center*
  Designer Kristin Odermatt
15.
  Client   *Salus Media*
  Designers Tracy Moon, Amy Gustincic
16.
  Client   *Cedars-Sinai Medical Center*
  Designers Diane Kuntz, Sherry Caris

1.

COLOR-TEX
I N T E R N A T I O N A L

2.

BESTFOODS

3.

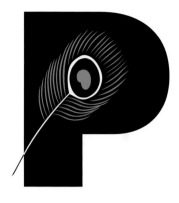

4.

KEMPER FUNDS

5.

Beyond
Boxes

6.

7.

CONSECO

8.

9.

10.

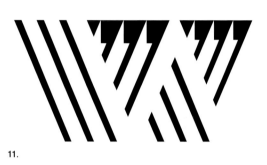

11.

OBJECT WARE

12.

13.

LOCKHEED MARTIN

14.

Spectrum HoloByte

15.

1, 2, 4, 7, 10
Design Firm **Doerr Associates**
3, 5, 8, 13, 14
Design Firm **Enterprise IG**
6, 9, 12, 15
Design Firm **Triad, Inc.**
11
Design Firm **360 Design Assoc.**

1.
Client   *Peacock Products*
Designer   Priscilla White Sturges

2.
Client   *Color-Tex International*
Designer   Priscilla White Sturges

3.
Client   *Bestfoods*
Design Director
         Eugene J. Grossman
Designer   Steve Cazlan

4.
Client   *Insight Partners Inc.*
Designer   Priscilla White Sturges

5.
Client   *Kemper Funds*
Creative Director
         William Ayres
Designer   Wendy Squires

6.
Client   *DSC Communications*
Designer   Michael Dambrowski,
         Carol Hoover

7.
Client   *Righter Corporation*
Designer   Priscilla White Sturges

8.
Client   *Conseco*
Director   William Ayres
Designer   Sally Hwang

9.
Client   *Fisk Communications*
Designer   Michael Dambrowski

10.
Client   *York Spiral Stairs*
Designer   Priscilla White Sturges

11.
Client   *D.L. White Builders*
Designers   Howard Sturges,
         Priscilla White Sturges

12.
Client   *ObjectWare*
Designer   Michael Hinshaw

13.
Client   *Hilton Hotels*
Creative Director
         Gene Grossman
Designer   Aere Cazlau

14.
Client   *Lockheed Martin*
Creative Director
         Gene Grossman
Designer   Bob Wily

15.
Client   *Spectrum HoloByte*
Designers   Richard Wilson, Carol Hoover

1.

Wienstroer Painting

2.

3.

4.

Hertz
Claim Management

5.

OPTIMUM GROUP
Marketing & Visual Communications Solutions

6.

7.

Downtown
B R O O K L Y N

8.

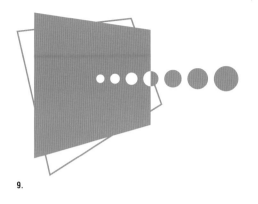

9.

10.

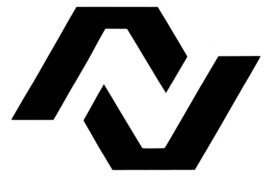

11.

12.

ONE
PENN
PLAZA

13.

NETAC

14.

15.

1.

2.

BUFFALO™

FRANCISCAN
INSTITUTE

3.

4.

Reaching
out,
one
to another

5.

6.

7.

Buffalo Arts Studio

8.

306

9.

10.

helena pentathlon

11.

12.

International Filler Corporation

14.

13.

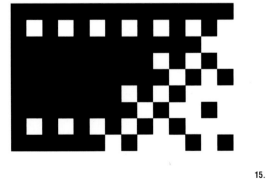

15.

1, 4, 6, 11, 15
Design Firm **Edward Walter Design**
2, 3, 7-10, 12-14
Design Firm **Crowley Webb And Associates**
5
Design Firm **HDS Marcomm**
1.
Client   *Jacobs Gardner Office Supply*
Designer   Edward Walter
2.
Client   *Greater Buffalo Convention & Visitors Bureau*
Designer   Rob Wynne
3.
Client   *Franciscan Institute*
Designer   Dion Pender
4.
Client   *Pace Development*
Designer   Edward Walter
5.
Client   *Hitachi Data Systems*
Designer   Kim Haley
6.
Client   *Hugh Browne*
Designer   Martin Brynell

7.
Client   *Brimm's Inc.*
Designer   Dave Buck
8.
Client   *Buffalo Arts Studio*
Designer & Art Director
             Brian Grunert
9.
Client   *Mount Mercy Academy*
Designer   Dion Pender
10.
Client   *Crowley Webb And Associates*
Designer   Dave Buck
11.
Client   *AirSystems, Inc.*
Designer   Edward Walter
12.
Client   *Helena Pentathlon*
Designer   Dion Pender
13.
Client   *Brimm's Inc.*
Designer   Dave Buck
14.
Client   *International Filler*
Designer   John Webb
15.
Client   *National Digital Corporation*
Designer   Edward Walter

307

1.

2.

ATTICUS

3.

The Davis Academy

4.

5.

6.

7.

8.

BUCKHEAD
PLAZA

9.

10.

11.

Community
Savings

12.

13.

14.

15.

(all)		
Design Firm	**Rousso+Associates, Inc.**	
Designer	Steven B. Rousso	
1.		
Client	*Brownlee Jewelers*	
2.		
Client	*The Atticus Group*	
3.		
Client	*The Davis Academy*	
4.		
Client	*Demand Products*	
5.		
Client	*Buffington & Lloyd*	
6.		
Client	*Centennial American Properties, Ltd.*	
7.		
Client	*Georgia Power Company*	

8.	
Client	*Circle 75 Office Park*
9.	
Client	*Taylor Mathis*
10.	
Client	*David's Ltd.*
11.	
Client	*Atlanta International Airport*
12.	
Client	*Community Savings*
13.	
Client	*Digital Controls*
14.	
Client	*Corporate Resource Development*
15.	
Client	*Software Solutions*

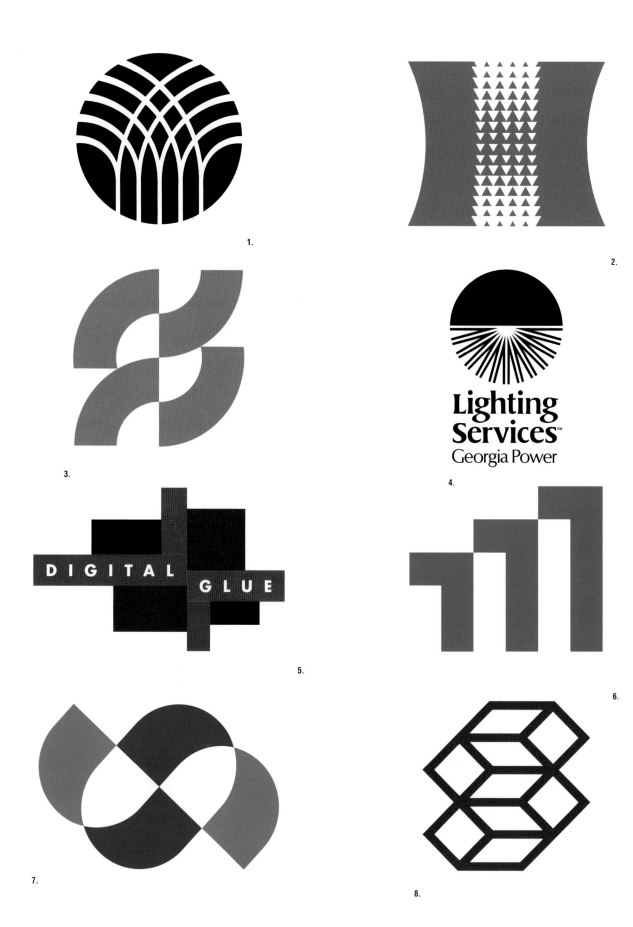

1.

2.

3.

Lighting
Services℠
Georgia Power

4.

DIGITAL GLUE

5.

6.

7.

8.

9.

10.

11.

12.

13.

14.

15.

(all)			**8.**	
Design Firm	**Rousso+Associates, Inc.**		Client	Southern Engineering Company
Designer	Steven B. Rousso		**9.**	
1.			Client	Lotus Carpets
Client	Childress Klein Properties		**10.**	
2.			Client	The Metro Companies
Client	Harbinger Corporation		**11.**	
3.			Client	OmniOffices
Client	Ferguson Enterprises		**12.**	
4.			Client	International Banking Technologies
Client	Georgia Power Company		**13.**	
5.			Client	Rousso+Associates, Inc.
Client	Digital Glue		**14.**	
6.			Client	VIDA
Client	The Metro Companies		**15.**	
7.			Client	The West Corporation
Client	Callaway Carpet Co.			

1.

2.

3.

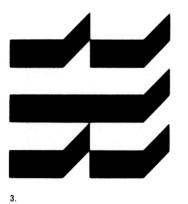

GENUARDI'S

FAMILY MARKETS

4.

3G DESIGN & ILLUSTRATION

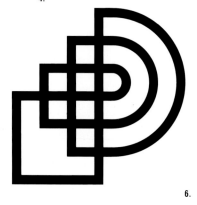

5.

6.

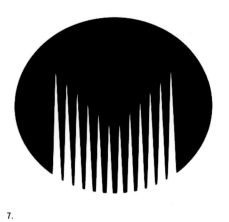

7.

DALLAS ZOO

8.

312

9.

10.

11.

12.

13.

TELE**S**UITE

14.

15.

313

1, 6, 10, 13
Design Firm **Rousso+Associates, Inc.**
Designer Steven B. Rousso
2, 3, 7-9, 11, 12, 15
Design Firm **RBMM/The Richards Group**
4
Design Firm **3G Design & Illustration**
5, 14
Design Firm **Design Forum**
1.
 Client *Airtouch Cellular*
2.
 Client *Summerfield*
 Designer RBMM
3.
 Client *Hill*
 Designer D.C. Stipp
4.
 Client *3G Design & Illustration*
 Designer Grant Guinouard
5.
 Client *Genuardi's Family Markets*
 Designer Carolyn Wiedeman
6.
 Client *Peterson Properties*

7.
 Client *Metrocel*
 Designer Steve Miller
8.
 Client *Dallas Zoo*
 Designer Dick Mitchell
9.
 Client *Stoneridge*
 Designer RBMM
10.
 Client *Jordan Properties*
11.
 Client *Bear Creek Wood Works*
 Designer Jackson Wang
12.
 Client *MIxon Enterprises & Mixon Investments*
 Designer RBMM
13.
 Client *Locations South*
14.
 Client *Telesuite*
Senior Graphic Designer
 Amy McCombs
 Designer Ken Cheney
15.
 Client *Execucom*
 Designer Brian Boyd

1.

2.

3.

4.

5.

COFFEEHOUSE 98

6.

7.

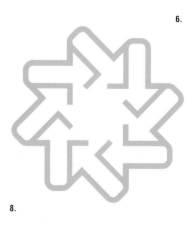

8.

9.

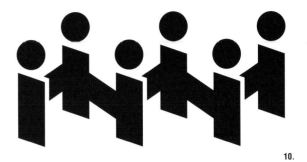

10.

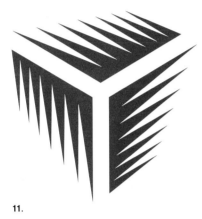

11.

12.

13.

14.

15.

1.

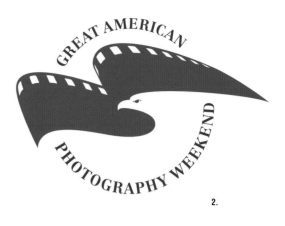

GREAT AMERICAN PHOTOGRAPHY WEEKEND

2.

3.

4.

CITYPLACE

5.

THE LIBRARY

6.

HONEY AND EGGI

7.

PUBLIC EXECUTIONS

8.

316

9.

10.

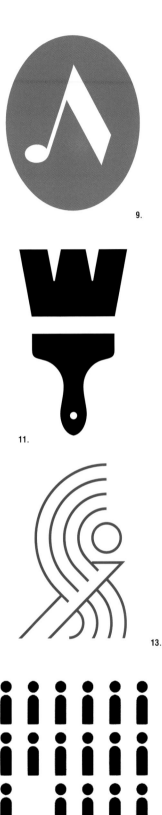

11.

Alice's Handweaving

12.

REUNION

14.

13.

i i i i i i
i i i i i i
i . i i i i

KIDFEST

15.

1, 4, 5, 7-11, 14, 15
  Design Firm **RBMM/The Richards Group**

2, 3, 6, 12, 13
  Design Firm **Kirby Stephens Design, Inc.**

1.
  Client   *Tom Thumb - Page*
  Designer Dick Mitchell
2.
  Client   *Great American Photography*
           Weekend
  Designers Kirby Stephens, Bill Jones
3.
  Client   *Lake Cumberland Performing Arts*
  Designer Kirby Stephens
4.
  Client   *Sell Track*
  Designer Dick Mitchell
5.
  Client   *Southland Corporation*
  Designer RBMM
6.
  Client   *Pulaski County Public Library*
  Designer Bill Jones

7.
  Client   *Earth Grains*
  Designer RBMM
8.
  Client   *Public Executions*
  Designer Jackson Wang
9.
  Client   *Aldredge Music Supply*
  Designer Luis Ascevedo
10.
  Client   *Oryx Energy*
  Designer Steve Miller
11.
  Client   *Willis Painting*
  Designer D.C. Stipp
12.
  Client   *Alice's Handweaving*
  Designer Bill Jones
13.
  Client   *Sterling Imaging Radiology*
           & Mammography
  Designer Bill Jones
14.
  Client   *Reunion Arena*
  Designer RBMM
15.
  Client   *Kidfest*
  Designer D.C. Stipp

1.

2.

3.

4.

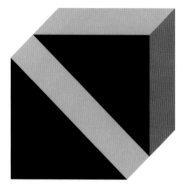

D

Dallas Public Schools

5.

6.

7.

8.

9.

10.

11.

12.

13.

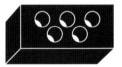

Adopt An Olympic Brick

14.

15.

(all)
Design Firm **RBMM/The Richards Group**

1.
Client *Team Mad Dog*
Designer RBMM

2.
Client *The Family Place*
Designer Brian Boyd

3.
Client *Norris*
Designer RBMM

4.
Client *Dr. Saretsky*
Designer Luis Ascevedo

5.
Client *Dallas Public Schools*
Designer Dick Mitchell

6.
Client *Mobility*
Designer Steve Miller

7.
Client *Hearts & Hammers*
Designer Dick Mitchell

8.
Client *The Dallas Symphony Orchestra*
Designer Horacio Cobos

9.
Client *Amerifest*
Designer Horacio Cobos

10.
Client *Central American*
Designer Horacio Cobos

11.
Client *Facial Aesthetic Systems*
Designer Luis Ascevedo

12.
Client *Head Golf*
Designer Horacio Cobos

13.
Client *Film Casters*
Designer Dick Mitchell

14.
Client *Home Depot*
Designer Kenny Garrison

15.
Client *Lewisville Humane Society*
Designer Luis Ascevedo

319

1.

2.
CRESCENT

3.
KPT
Kentucky Physical Therapy

4.

5.
DECADE

6.
VITALLY

7.
THE CENTER
For Rural Development

8.
ALUMITECH

Harald Sund/photographer

9.

10.

11.

McCLOREY
LAW OFFICES

12.

ANDE MAC DESIGN

13.

14.

15.

1, 3, 7, 8, 10, 12, 14, 15
Design Firm **Kirby Stephens Design, Inc.**
2, 6, 9, 13
Design Firm **Walsh & Associates, Inc.**
4, 5, 11
Design Firm **RBMM/The Richards Group**

1.
Client *Tater Knob Pottery & Farm*
Designer William V. Cox
2.
Client *Crescent Foods*
Designers Frederick Walsh, Miriam Lisco
3.
Client *Kentucky Physical Therapy*
Designer William V. Cox
4.
Client *Leadership Network*
Designer Jackson Wang
5.
Client *Episcopal School of Dallas*
Designer Brian Boyd
6.
Client *Vitalli*
Designer Miriam Lisco
Calligrapher Glenn Yoshiyama

7.
Client *The Center For Rural Development*
Designer Bill Jones
8.
Client *Alumitech, Inc.*
Designers Bill Jones, Kirby Stephens
9.
Client *Harald Sund Photographer*
Designer Miriam Lisco
10.
Client *Fire and Clay Pottery*
Designer Kirby Stephens
11.
Client *The Greater Dallas Chamber*
Designer Steve Miller
12.
Client *John McClorey*
Designer William V. Cox
13.
Client *Ande Mac Design*
Designer Miriam Lisco
14.
Client *Amon's Bakery*
Designer Kirby Stephens
15.
Client *One World Software*
Designer William V. Cox

1.

2.

3.

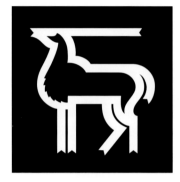

4.

5.

6.

7.

8.

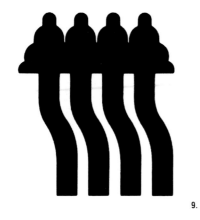

9.

10.

11.

12.

13.

14.

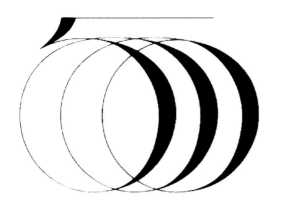

15.

1, 6, 10, 13
  Design Firm **Walsh & Associates, Inc.**
2-5, 7-9, 11, 12, 14, 15
  Design Firm **RBMM/The Richards Group**
1.
  Client   *Northstar Cold Storage*
  Designers   Miriam Lisco, Katie Dolejsi
2.
  Client   *Pinewild*
  Designer   RBMM
3.
  Client   *Cantina Laredo*
  Designer   RBMM
4.
  Client   *Wellington Publishing*
  Designer   Dick Mitchell
5.
  Client   *Argo*
  Designer   Brian Boyd
6.
  Client   *Concord Mortgage*
  Designer   Miriam Lisco

7.
  Client   *Bridge To Life*
  Designer   RBMM
8.
  Client   *Verdi*
  Designer   Luis Ascevedo
9.
  Client   *The Trails*
  Designer   RBMM
10.
  Client   *Washington Cheese*
  Designer   Miriam Lisco
  Illustrator Larry Jost
11.
  Client   *Hope Cottage Adoption Center*
  Designer   RBMM
12.
  Client   *Aubrey Hair*
  Designer   RBMM
13.
  Client   *Shoalwater Bay Oyster Co.*
  Designer   Miriam Lisco
14.
  Client   *WFAN (New York)*
  Designer   RBMM
15.
  Client   *The 500 Inc.*
  Designer   D.C. Stipp

1.

2.

3.

4.

5.

6.

7.

8.

9.

10.

11.

12.

13.

14.

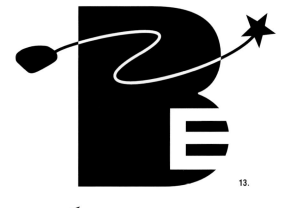

E L E C T R I C

15.

16.

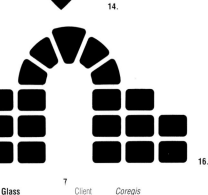

17.

1.

2.

Design/Build Construction

3.

4.

5.

ALLIANCE
FOR GROWTH AND PROGRESS

6.

7.

1, 2, 4, 5, 7
Design Firm **Lipson • Alport • Glass & Associates**
3, 6
Design Firm **Miller & White Advertising**
1.
Client   *Tyndar House Publishers (New Living Translation)*
Designer Lipson • Alport • Glass & Associates
2.
Client   *Lipson • Alport • Glass & Associates*
Designers Tracy Bacilek, Sam Ciuus
3.
Client   *Garmong Design/Build Construction*
Designer Bill White

4.
Client   *Jockey*
Designers Tracy Bacilek, Carol Davis, Amy Russell
5.
Client   *Kraft Foods, Inc. (Maxwell House)*
Designer Lipson • Alport • Glass & Associates
6.
Client   *Alliance for Growth & Progress*
Designer Scott Lee
7.
Client   *S.C. Johnson & Sons*
Designer Lipson • Alport • Glass & Associates
(opposite)
Client   *Scott Paper Company*
Design Firm **Lipson • Alport • Glass & Associates**
Designer Lori Cerwin

1.

2.

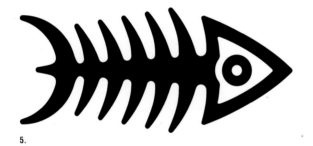

3.

4.

5.

6.

7.

8.

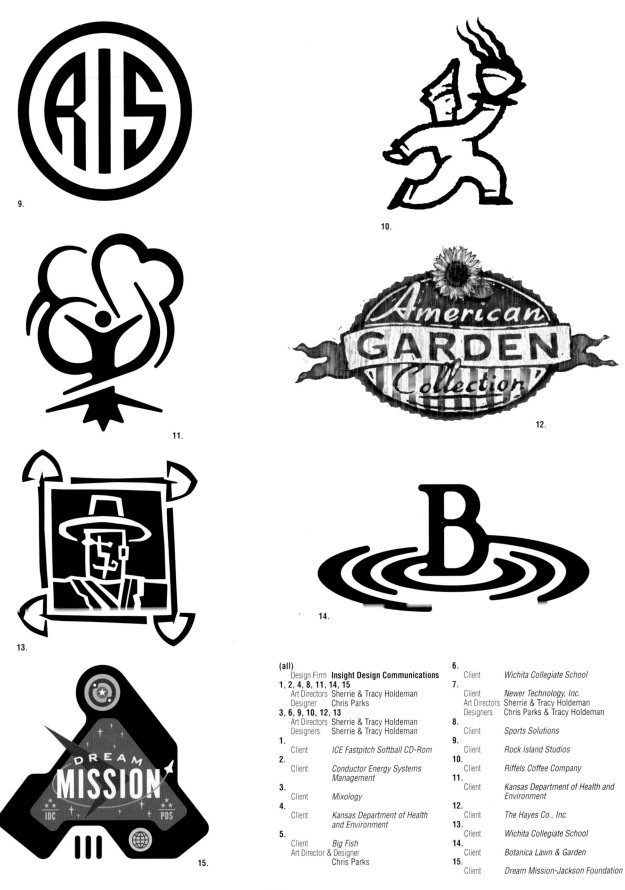

9.

10.

11.

12.

13.

14.

15.

(all)
Design Firm **Insight Design Communications**
1, 2, 4, 8, 11, 14, 15
  Art Directors Sherrie & Tracy Holdeman
  Designer Chris Parks
3, 6, 9, 10, 12, 13
  Art Directors Sherrie & Tracy Holdeman
  Designers Sherrie & Tracy Holdeman
1.
  Client *ICE Fastpitch Softball CD-Rom*
2.
  Client *Conductor Energy Systems Management*
3.
  Client *Mixology*
4.
  Client *Kansas Department of Health and Environment*
5.
  Client *Big Fish*
  Art Director & Designer
          Chris Parks

6.
  Client *Wichita Collegiate School*
7.
  Client *Newer Technology, Inc.*
  Art Directors Sherrie & Tracy Holdeman
  Designers Chris Parks & Tracy Holdeman
8.
  Client *Sports Solutions*
9.
  Client *Rock Island Studios*
10.
  Client *Riffels Coffee Company*
11.
  Client *Kansas Department of Health and Environment*
12.
  Client *The Hayes Co., Inc.*
13.
  Client *Wichita Collegiate School*
14.
  Client *Botanica Lawn & Garden*
15.
  Client *Dream Mission-Jackson Foundation*

1.

DAWN OF THE NEW CENTURY

2.

MILLENNIUM
DESIGN

3.

4.

5.

6.

7.

NAIAD
TECHNOLOGIES, INC.

8.

332

DREAMIN' 1993

9.

10.

11.

12.

13.

14.

15.

1, 4-7, 10, 11, 13-15
Design Firm **Insight Design Communications**
Art Directors Sherrie & Tracy Holdeman
2, 8, 9
Design Firm **Young & Roehr, Inc.**
3
Design Firm **Millennium Design**
12
Design Firm **Bonnell Design Associates**
1.
Client *Art Effects*
Designers Sherrie & Tracy Holdeman
2.
Client *Freightliner Trucks*
Designer Martin Rupert
3.
Client *Millennium Design*
Designer Michele LaPointe
4.
Client *LD Supply*
Designer Chris Parks
5.
Client *Chalet Sports Bar and Grill*
Designer Chris Parks
6.
Client *Swan Brothers Dairy, Inc.*
Designers Sherrie & Tracy Holdeman

7.
Client *The Hayes Company -
Chef's Herb Garden TM*
Designers Sherrie & Tracy Holdeman
8.
Client *Naiad Technologies, Inc.*
Designer Amy Keck
9.
Client *Freightliner Used Trucks*
Designer Martin Rupert
10.
Client *Prairie Print*
Designers Sherrie & Tracy Holdeman
11.
Client *Old Town Association of Wichita*
Designer Chris Parks
12.
Client *La Belle Maison*
Designer Miyako Taguchi
13.
Client *Rock Island Studios*
Designers Sherrie & Tracy Holdeman
14.
Client *Mental Health Association
of Kansas*
Designers Sherrie & Tracy Holdeman
15.
Client *No Tomorrow*
Designers Sherrie & Tracy Holdeman

JAVAWORKS

FLYING MULE COFFEE

A KICKASS BREW

DURANGO, COLORADO

1.

2.

THE STABLES

WORKS

TALENT THAT WORKS

3.

4.

FAIR SAINT LOUIS

5.

MARKETING

SOLUTIONS

STRATEGIC

20/20

SOLUTIONS
DELIVERING

RESULTS

6.

7.

era

8.

334

9.

10.

11.

12.

13.

14.

15.

1, 4, 5, 8, 10, 11, 14
   Design Firm **Bartels & Company, Inc.**
2, 3, 6, 7, 9, 12, 13, 15
   Design Firm **Insight Design Communications**
   Art Directors Sherrie & Tracy Holdeman
1.
   Client   *Javaworks*
   Designer David Bartels
2.
   Client   *McMinimy Photography*
   Designers Sherrie & Tracy Holdeman
3.
   Client   *The Stables*
   Designers Sherrie & Tracy Holdeman
4.
   Client   *The Genesis Institute*
   Designers Ron Rodemacher, David Bartels
5.
   Client   *Fair St. Louis Organization*
   Designers Bob Thomas, David Bartels
6.
   Client   *20/20 Solutions*
   Designers Sherrie & Tracy Holdeman

7.
   Client   *Solid Solutions*
   Designers Sherrie & Tracy Holdeman
8.
   Client   *ERA GSM*
   Designers David Bartels, Brian Barclay
9.
   Client   *Big Dog Custom Motorcycles Inc.*
   Designers Sherrie & Tracy Holdeman
10.
   Client   *Deltalog*
   Designers Brian Barclay, David Bartels
11.
   Designer David Bartels, Brian Barclay
12.
   Client   *Association of Blockbuster*
            Franchisees
   Designer Chris Parks
13.
   Client   *WouArts*
            (Women of Untraditional Arts)
   Designers Sherrie & Tracy Holdeman
14.
   Client   *Quantitative Capital Partners*
   Designers David Bartels, Ron Rodemacher
15.
   Client   *Newer Technology, Inc.*
   Designers Chris Parks, Tracy Holdeman

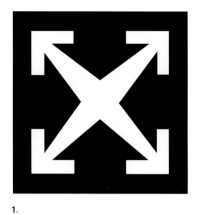

1.

2.

3.

4.

5.

6.

7.

8.

PEACHWOOD
MEDICAL GROUP

9.

10.

11.

12.

QuadraSeps

13.

14.

15.

1, 4, 5, 7, 10, 11, 14, 15
Design Firm **Insight Design Communications**
Art Directors & Designers
         Sherrie & Tracy Holdeman
2, 3, 6, 8, 9, 12, 13
Design Firm **Shields Design**

1.
  Client   *Interex*
2.
  Client   *Maxim Mortgage Corporation*
  Designer Charles Shields
3.
  Client   *The Ken Roberts Company*
  Designer Charles Shields
  Illustrator Doug Hansen
4.
  Client   *Fresh Paint*
5.
  Client   *Kicks*
6.
  Client   *Keiser Sports*
  Designer Charles Shields

7.
  Client   *Twin Valley*
8.
  Client   *The Ken Roberts Company*
  Designer Charles Shields
  Illustrator Doug Hansen
9.
  Client   *Revell & Associates*
  Designer Charles Shields
10.
  Client   *Network Interface Corporation*
11.
  Client   *Hastings Filters Inc.*
12.
  Client   *Great Pacific Trading Company*
  Designer Charles Shields
  Illustrator Doug Hansen
13.
  Client   *QuadraSeps*
  Art Director Charles Shields
  Designer Juan Vega
14.
  Client   *Timberline Steakhouse & Grill*
15.
  Client   *Tortilla Factory*

Tanya's SOUP KITCHEN

1.

ALISTAR
INSURANCE, INC.

2.

3.

4.

5.

7.

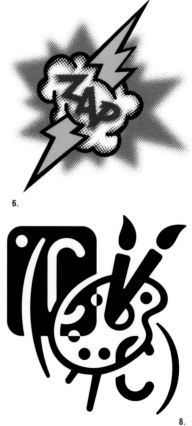

8.

9.

10.

11.

12.

13.

14.

CROWN
PRINTING

15.

1, 4-8, 10, 11, 13, 14
Design Firm **Insight Design Communications**
Art Directors Sherrie & Tracy Holdeman
2, 3, 9, 12, 15
Design Firm **Shields Design**
1.
 Client Tanya's Soup Kitchen
 Designers Sherrie Holdeman,
 Tracy Holdeman, Chris Parks
2.
 Client Alistar Insurance, Inc.
 Art Director Charles Shields
 Designer Laura Thornton
3.
 Client Valley Fresh Produce
 Designer Charles Shields
 Illustrator Jane Bowden
4.
 Client Holdeman's Total Lawn
 Care Service
 Designers Sherrie & Tracy Holdeman
5.
 Client Kara
 Designer Sherrie & Tracy Holdeman
6.
 Client Grene Vision Group -
 Zap Promotion
 Designer Chris Parks

7.
 Client World Fitness, Inc.
 Designers Sherrie & Tracy Holdeman
8.
 Client COMCARE of Sedgwick County
 Designer Chris Parks
9.
 Client Attitude Online
 Art Director Charles Shields
 Designer Juan Vega
10.
 Client The Hayes Company, Inc.
 Designers Sherrie & Tracy Holdeman
11.
 Client Virtual Celebrity Productions
 Designers Sherrie & Tracy Holdeman
12.
 Client Main Street Trading Company
 Designer Charles Shields
 Illustrator David Wariner
13.
 Client Jitters
 Designers Sherrie & Tracy Holdeman
14.
 Client Grene Vision Group -
 Eye Care on Call
 Designers Sherrie & Tracy Holdeman
15.
 Client Crown Printing
 Designer Charles Shields

1.

2.

HealthComp

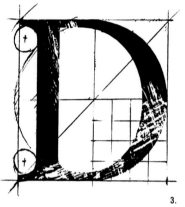

3.

4.

5.

6.

7.

8.

340

ValliWide Bank℠

9.

10.

THE **PURPLE** MOON
DANCE PROJECT

12.

11.

topo

13.

Phil   *Rudy*

Photography

14

SPORT
SLING

15.

341

1.

2.

3.

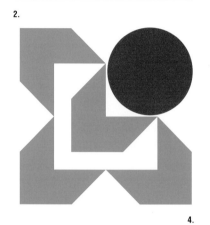

4.

5.

6.

7.

8.

342

9.

10.

The Shubert Organization

11.

12.

13.

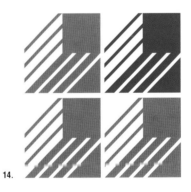

14.

RESTAURANT & BAR

15.

343

1, 7, 10, 15
Design Firm **Jeff Fisher LogoMotives**
2, 6, 9, 13
Design Firm **Insight Design Communications**
Art Directors Sherrie & Tracy Holdeman
3, 5, 8, 12, 14
Design Firm **Taylor & Ives Incorporated**
4, 11
Design Firm **Fujita Design, Inc.**

1.
Client *Samuels Yoelin Kantor Seymour & Spinrad LLP*
Designer Jeff Fisher
2.
Client *Raytheon Corporation*
Designers Sherrie & Tracy Holdeman
3.
Client *Bankers Trust Company/ Globe Set*
Designer Alisa Zamir
4.
Client *Vanguard Fruit Company*
Designer Alisa Zamir
5.
Client *TIG Holdings, Inc.*
Designer Alisa Zamir

6.
Client *Cityarts*
Designer Chris Parks
7.
Client *Ed Cunningham*
Designer Jeff Fisher
8.
Client *New York Stock Exchange*
Designer Alisa Zamir
9.
Client *Love Box Company*
Designers Sherrie & Tracy Holdeman
10.
Client *Samuels & Nudelman*
Designer Jeff Fisher
11.
Client *The Shubert Organization*
Designer Alisa Zamir
12.
Client *NaPro BioTherapeutics, Inc.*
Designers Alisa Zamir, Martin Fujita
13.
Client *Massco*
Designer Chris Parks
14.
Client *Somerset*
Designer Alisa Zamir
15.
Client *Indies Restaurant & Bar*
Designer Jeff Fisher

1.

2.
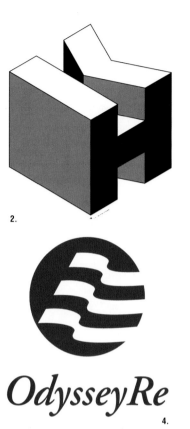

3.

4.
OdysseyRe

5.
S^tARS

6.

7.
BROCK

8.
U. G. L. Y.
BARTENDER
CONTEST

9.

10.

double entendre

11.

12.

13.

14.

EVENTX

15.

1, 4, 5, 10, 12
Design Firm **Taylor & Ives Incorporated**
2
Design Firm **RVI Corporation**
3, 6, 7, 13, 15
Design Firm **Identity Center**
8, 9, 11
Design Firm **Double Entendre**
14
Design Firm **DLS Design**

1.
Client   *Adler & Shaykin*
Designer   Alisa Zamir
2.
Client   *Klein and Hoffman Inc.*
Designer   Wayne Kosterman
3.
Client   *American Security Mortgage*
Designer   Wayne Kosterman
4.
Client   *Odyssey Reinsurance Corporation*
Designer   Alisa Zamir
5.
Client   *Price Waterhouse LLP*
Designers   Alisa Zamir, Daniel Caspescha
6.
Client   *Wrightwood Industries*
Designers   Wayne Kosterman, Darin Hasley,
Jason Blaskovich

7.
Client   *Brock Software Products*
Designer   Wayne Kosterman
8.
Client   *Western Washington Multiple
Sclerosis Society*
Designers   Richard A. Smith, Daniel P. Smith
9.
Client   *SheWear*
Designers   Richard A. Smith, Daniel P. Smith
10.
Client   *RCG Information Technology*
Designer   Alisa Zamir
11.
Client   *Double Entendre*
Designers   Richard A. Smith, Daniel P. Smith
12.
Client   *International Depository &
Clearing Inc.*
Designers   Alisa Zamir, Kurt Jennings
13.
Client   *Premier Banks*
Designer   Wayne Kosterman
14.
Client   *Offline Media (Webmark)*
Designer   David Schiffer
15.
Client   *Eventx Imagemakers*
Designer   Darin Hasley

THERMOLASE
C O R P O R A T I O N

1.

2.

 Little Kids™

3.

TG**R** TOLL GATE
RADIOLOGY INC.

4.

INSTIN**::**T

5.

 **Rockwell**

6.

K**M**C Telecom

7.

 EcotritionFoods™
healthy foods for a healthy planet

8.

POS**T**IM**E**

9.

L E P R E
Physical Therapy

10.

eagle eye   11.

IntelliGenetics   12.

GRAND
AIRE
EXPRESS   13.

COFFEE KIDS™

GROUNDS FOR HOPE   14.

15.

JOBPRO

FLEXIBLE STAFFING SOLUTIONS   17.

16.

18.

1
  Design Firm **Maddocks & Company**
2, 13
  Design Firm **Schlatter Design**
3, 4, 8, 10, 14-17
  Design Firm **Creative Vision Design Co.**
  Designer Gregory Gonsalves
5, 6
  Design Firm **Yuguchi Group, Inc.**
7
  Design Firm **Emphasis Seven
    Communications, Inc.**
9
  Design Firm **RMI, Inc.**
11, 12
  Design Firm **Philip Quinn & Partners**
  Designer Philip Quinn
16
  Design Firm **Diane Kuntz Design**
1.
  Client *Thermolase Corporation*
  Creative Director
        Mary Scott
  Designers Camille Favilli, Carrie Dobbel
2.
  Client *Axiom Communications*
  Designers Richard Schlatter, Frederick
        DeRuiter
3.
  Client *Little Kids, Inc.*
4.
  Client *Toll Gate Radiology*

5.
  Client *Instinet*
  Designer Clifford Yuguchi
6.
  Client *Rockwell*
7.
  Client *KMC Telecom*
  Designer Debra Nemeth
8.
  Client *Ecotrition Foods*
9.
  Client *Saab Cars USA, Inc.*
  Designer Lee Einhorn
10.
  Client *Lepre Physical Therapy*
11.
  Client *Eagle Eye*
12.
  Client *IntelliGenetics, Inc.*
13.
  Client *Grand Aire Express*
  Designer Richard Schlatter
14.
  Client *Coffee Kids*
15.
  Client *Rick Sippel/Sippel Photography*
16.
  Client *Hidden Valley Ranch*
  Designers Diane Kuntz, Marneu`Jameson
17.
  Client *Jobpro*
18.
  Client *Pizzeria Uno*

1.

2.

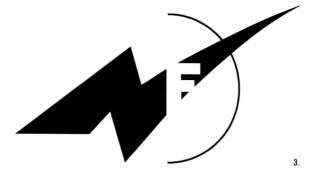

3.

4.

5.

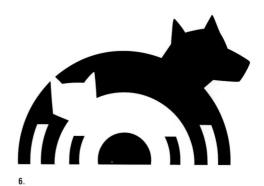

6.

7.

1
Design Firm **DeMartino Design**
2, 3, 6, 7
Design Firm **Graphic Design Continuum**
4, 5
Design Firm **Dennis S. Juett & Associates Inc.**

1.
Client   *Haynes Security Inc.*
Designer Erick DeMartino
2.
Client   *Paradigm*
Designer John Emery
3.
Client   *New Futures of Dayton*
Designer John Emery
4.
Client   *TransWorld Video Lab, Inc.*
Designers Jeffrey Lawson, Dennis S. Juett

5.
Client   *The Graphics Shop*
Designer Dennis Scott Juett
6.
Client   *Humane Society of Greater Dayton*
Designer Danielle Dumont
7.
Client   *Victoria Theatre Association (Camp Victoria)*
Designer Danielle Dumont
(opposite)
Client   *FAO Schwarz*
Design Firm **Walker Group/CNI**
Designers Sandra Hagashi, Edwin Sierra

1.

2.

TRUSTEC

3.

4.

Vaughan Walls

5.

NORTHWEST
VENDINGCO.

6.

Delta Cove
T O W N H O M E S

7.

BIODYNE

8.

350

Huntington Hospital
9.

10.

JULIAN HARO
12.

OXFORD
CLINIC
11.

ΛRΓS
14.

ALPINE PRESS
INCORPORATED
13.

AVIALL
15.

1
Design Firm **Nuts and Bolts Design**
2, 3, 4, 6, 7, 9, 15
Design Firm **Dennis S. Juett & Associates Inc.**
5, 8, 12, 13
Design Firm **Lincoln Design**
10
Design Firm **Niedermeier Design**
11, 14
Design Firm **Peg Faimon Design**

1.
Client *Nuts and Bolts Design*
Designer Kurt Niedermeier
2.
Client *TRUSTEC*
Designer Dennis S. Juett
3.
Client *SHIELD Healthcare Centers*
Designer Dennis Scott Juett
4.
Client *Vaughan Walls, Inc.*
Designer Dennis S. Juett
5.
Client *PepsiCo of Eugene*
Designer Thomas Lincoln
6.
Client *Delta Cove Townhomes*
Designer Dennis S. Juett

7.
Client *Biodyne*
Designers Dennis S. Juett, Jeffrey Lawson
8.
Client *Ceruzzi Properties*
Designer Thomas Lincoln
9.
Client *Huntington Memorial Hospital*
Designers Robert Blatherwick, Dennis S. Juett
10.
Client *Echo Falls*
Designer Kurt Niedermeier
11.
Client *Oxford Clinic*
Designer Peg Faimon
12.
Client *Julian Haro*
Designer Thomas Lincoln
13.
Client *Alpine Press*
Designer Thomas Lincoln
14.
Client *Miami University
School of Fine Arts*
Designer Peg Faimon
15.
Client *AVIALL*
Designers Dennis S. Juett, Dan Hanrahan

Midtown
Pointe

1.

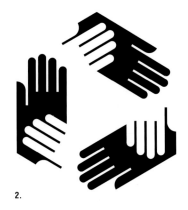

2.

3.

ALLIANCE FOR HEALTH

4.

5.

DesignPartnership

6.

7.

8.

9.

MacIlwinen
Development, Inc.

10.

Crisp
Hughes
Evans
LLP

11.

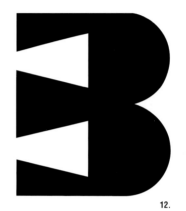

12.

LEADERSHIP GREER

13.

14.

15.

1.

2.

3.

MaguirePhotographics

4.

5.

Z

6.

7.

Greer

Greater Greer Development Corporation

8.

GOLFDOME
THE ULTIMATE DRIVING RANGE

9.

Boutique
EUROPA

10.

11.

12.

GSPAIRPORT
I N T E R N A T I O N A L

13.

14.

15.

16.

17.

SELECTS

1.

RED PEPPA ™

2.

S·KYLINE
ENTERPRISES

3.

WESTHOUSE
DESIGN

4.

DigiTech
Software Duplication

5.

GATEWAY
INTERNATIONAL BUSINESS CENTER

6.

Pediatric HealthCare

7.

TIGER
TRANSPORT

8.

HITO
熱點

9.

Fueltrimmer

10.

356

OHIO MADE FILMS

11.

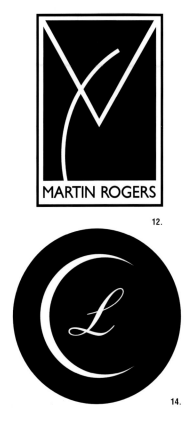

MARTIN ROGERS

12.

MEASURE

13.

14.

G

15.

O O O D C

De Colores

16.

THE PILLAR
OF SUPPORT
CAMPAIGN

17.

1.

SPIEGEL ELITE 2.

3.

4.

5.

The Wexan Group, Ltd. 6.

7.

8.

9.

THE BLACK BOOK 10.

11. Mattaliano

12. PLACE

13.

14.

15. Angotti/McHugh

16. AFOP

17. Globex

1, 4, 5, 8, 12, 13, 16
 Design Firm **Alphawave Designs**
2, 3, 6, 7, 9, 10, 11, 14, 15, 17
 Design Firm **Liska & Associates**

1.
 Client Division of Clinical Sciences, NCI
 Designer Douglas Dunbebin
2.
 Client Spiegel, Inc.
 Designers Staff
3.
 Client Frommer & Goldstein
 Designers Staff
4.
 Client World Kids Inc.
 Designer Douglas Dunbebin
5.
 Client Bonin & Associates
 Designer Douglas Dunbebin
6.
 Client The Wexan Group, Ltd.
 Designers Staff
7.
 Client Grainger
 Designers Staff
8.
 Client Alphawave Designs
 Designer Douglas Dunbebin

9.
 Client Elizabeth Zeschin Studio
 Designer Staff
10.
 Client Black Book
 Designer Steve Liska
11.
 Client Mattaliano
 Designer Marcos Chavez
12.
 Client N. E. Place/
   Matthews Media Group, Inc.
 Designer Douglas Dunbebin
13.
 Client National Hispanic Health Coalition
 Designer Douglas Dunbebin
14.
 Client Torchia Associates
 Designer Nancy Blackwell
15.
 Client Angotti/McHugh
 Designer Steve Liska
16.
 Client Association of Farmworker
   Opportunity Programs
 Designer Douglas Dunbebin
17.
 Client Chicago Mercantile Exchange
 Designer Steve Liska

1.

2.

3. INOCHI

4.

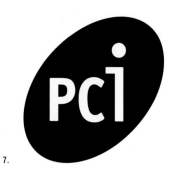

5.

6.

7.

8.

9.

10.

Maryland
Biotechnology
11. Institute

Fun in the Sun   12.

AcuStaf
13. C O R P O R A T I O N

14.

15.

16.

17.

1, 5, 12
Design Firm **Becker Design**
2, 9, 11
Design Firm **Dever Designs**
3, 6, 7, 14, 16
Design Firm **Liska & Associates**
4, 8, 13, 15, 17
Design Firm **Hedstrom/Blessing, Inc.**
10
Design Firm **Alphawave Designs**

1.
Client   *Ko-Thi Dance Company*
Designer   Neil Becker
2.
Client   *Mother Care*
Designers   Douglas Dunbebin, Jeff Dever
3.
Client   *Inochi*
Designer   Nancy Blackwell
4.
Client   *Target Stores*
Designer   Mike Goebel
5.
Client   *Charlton Photos Inc.*
Designer   Neil Becker
6.
Client   *Screenz*
Designers   Staff
7.
Client   *PCI Computers Limited*
Designer   Steve Liska

8.
Client   *Methodist Hospital Foundation*
Designer   Mike Goebel
9.
Client   *Camp Blue Ridge,*
   Potomac Conference of S.D.A.
Designers   Douglas Dunbebin, Jeff Dever
10.
Client   *Zack Fine Art Photography*
Designer   Douglas Dunbebin
11.
Client   *Maryland Biotechnology Institute*
Designers   Douglas Dunbebin, Jeffrey Dever
12.
Client   *Rite Hite Corporation*
Designer   Neil Becker
13.
Client   *AcuStaf Corporation*
Designer   Mike Goebel
14.
Client   *Chicago Symphony Orchestra*
Designer   Anne Schedler
15.
Client   *Lexington Square*
Designer   Mike Goebel
16.
Client   *Northern Possessions*
Designer   Anne Schedler
17.
Client   *St. Cloud Technical College*
Designer   Mike Goebel

1.

2. HealthLink

3. PetroCap

4.

5. GARDENSCAPES

6.

7. IREM

8.

9.

10. JOE LUNARDI ELECTRIC INCORPORATED

362

John Buck Company

11.

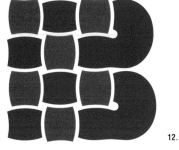

12.

13.

VIRTUEM
ENTERTAINMENT

14.

A M E R I C A N
CREW

15.

16.

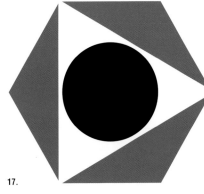

17.

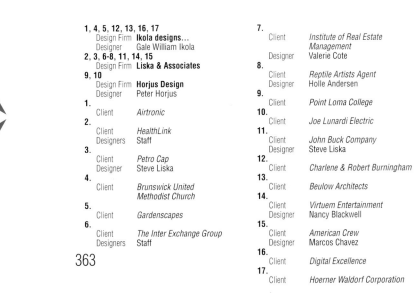

1.

2. Terra

3.

4. Territorial Savings

5. QNET

6. Uni·t·a·s
A TECHNICAL SERVICES GROUP

7. VOLK Packaging Corporation

8. OMAN

9. VKM

10. HD

364

11.

12.

13.

14.

15.

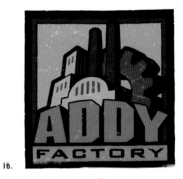

16.

17.

1, 2, 8, 9, 10
Design Firm **Liska & Associates**
3, 11
Design Firm **Ikola designs…**
Designer Gale William Ikola
4
Design Firm **Nick Kaars & Associates**
5
Design Firm **Cube Advertising & Design**
6, 7
Design Firm **Jasper & Bridge**
12
Design Firm **Scott Brown Design**
13, 14, 16
Design Firm **Dot Zero Design**
15, 17
Design Firm **ZGraphics, Ltd.**
Designer Gregg Rojewski

1.
Client *Learning Curve*
Designer Holle Anderson
2.
Client *Terra International*
Designer Steve Liska
3.
Client *Centennial Lakes Dental Group*
4.
Client *Territorial Savings*
Designers Nick Kaars & Fallon Lee
5.
Client *Nabanco, Inc.*
Designer David Chiow

6.
Client *Unitas*
Designer Andy Thorington
7.
Client *Volk Packaging Corporation*
Designers Alexander Bridge & Dan Howard
8.
Client *Oman*
Designer Steve Liska
9.
Client *Van Kampen Merritt*
Designer Steve Liska
10.
Client *Horticulture Design*
Designers Staff
11.
Client *Northern States Power Company*
12.
Designers Scott Brown, Janis Wong
13.
Client *Pioneer Balloon*
Designer Jon Wippich
14.
Client *Pioneer Balloon*
Designers Jon Wippich, Karen Wippich
15.
Client *Dundee Mainstreet*
16.
Client *Advertising Federation*
Designers Jon Wippich, Karen Wippich
17.
Client *Allen and Sons*

1.

2.

Welch Hydraulix

3.

A **PDR** Company

4.

5.

6.

7.

8.

9.

10.

366

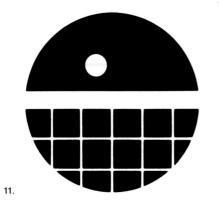

11.

MAKING SENSE OF IT

12.

13.

OUTRIGGER
Hotels Hawaii

14.

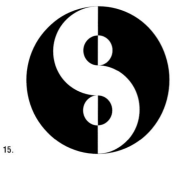

15.

Vaccinex ® LP
SCIENCE IN THE SERVICE OF MEDICINE

16.

KFWB
NEWS
98

17.

1.

THE SPORTS CLUB/LA

2.

ALPHA
FURNITURE
RESTORATION

3.

SUNSET

DECKS

4.

Ocean Pool

Bar & Grill

5.

[i]e design

6.

7.

five

visual communication
& design

8.

Financial Advisory Services

Providing Solutions

9.

Network World

World Class

10.

368

11.

SNEAKER
SISTERS
TM

12.

BELARIA

14.

R E L E A S E

S O F T W A R E

13.

F R A N C E S C A F R E E D M A N

S A N F R A N C I S C O

16.

C / L / B

15.

17.

1
   Design Firm **RTKL Associates Inc.**
2
   Design Firm **Cozad & Associates**
3, 4
   Design Firm **Kowalski Designworks, Inc.**
5, 13, 16, 17
   Design Firm **Arias Associates**
6
   Design Firm **IE Design**
7, 8
   Design Firm **Five Visual Communication
                 & Design**
9
   Design Firm **Communique**
10
   Design Firm **Horjus Design**
11
   Design Firm **Telesis**
12
   Design Firm **Diane Kuntz Design**
14, 15
   Design Firm **Susan Meshberg Graphic Design**

1.
   Client   *Burford Trocadero plc.*
   Designer   Glyn Rees
2.
   Client   *The Sports Club/LA*
   Designers Bryan Friel, Bob Cozad
3.
   Client   *Alpha Furniture Restoration*
   Designers Christine McFarren,
              Stephen Kowalski
4.
   Client   *Sunset Decks*
   Designers Camille Sauvé, Stephen Kowalski
5.
   Client   *Ocean Pool Bar & Grill,
              Four Seasons Aviara*
   Designers Mauricio Arias, Marcie Wilson
6.
   Client   *IE Design*
   Designer   Marcie Carson

7.
   Client   Mt. Auburn United Methodist Church
   Designers Rondi Tschopp, Danielle Fagan
8.
   Client   *Five Visual Communication
              & Design*
   Designers Rondi Tschopp, Danielle Fagan
9.
   Client   *Colarobba & Walliar*
   Designer   Tim Youngs
10.
   Client   *Network World*
   Designer   Peter Horjus
11.
   Client   *The Lacrosse Foundation*
   Designer   Frederick Kail
12.
   Client   *Sneaker Sisters*
   Designer   Diane Kuntz
13.
   Client   *Release Software*
   Designers Mauricio Arias, Steve Mortensen,
              Stephanie Yee
14.
   Client   *Bel Canto Fancy Foods Ltd.*
   Creative Director, Designer
              Susan Meshberg
15.
   Client   *Chateau Los Boldos (Chile)*
   Art Director, Designer
              Susan Meshberg
   Computer Artists
              Elaine MacFarlane, Jia Hwang
16.
   Client   *Francesca Freedman*
   Designers Mauricio Arias, Steve Mortensen,
              Vahn Phan
17.
   Client   *Apple Multimedia*
   Designer   Mauricio Arias

1.

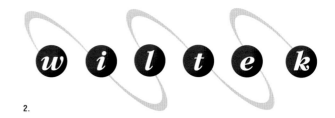

2.

CliniNet

3.

4.

5.

PNN

6.

7.

Strategic
Environmental
Management

8.

9.

Independent Weatherproofing Consultants, LLC

10.

11.

12.

13.

14.

15.

16.

17.

1		
	Design Firm	**Steven Guarnaccia**
2, 14		
	Design Firm	**The Wyant Simboli Group, Inc.**
3-6, 16, 17		
	Design Firm	**Paganucci Design, Inc.**
8		
	Design Firm	**Foth & Van Dyke**
9, 12		
	Design Firm	**Arias Associates**
	Designer	Mauricio Arias
10		
	Design Firm	**Allen Graphic Design**
11, 13, 15		
	Design Firm	**The Spangler Design Team**

1.
Client — *Steven Guarnaccia*
Designer — Steven Guarnaccia

2.
Client — *Wiltek Inc.*
Art Director — Julia Wyant
Designers — Ruth Teitlebaum, Kim Okosky, Julia Wyant

3.
Client — *Sandoz/Novartis*
Designer — Bob Paganucci

4.
Client — *The Child Care Company*
Designers — Bob Paganucci, Frank Paganucci

5.
Client — *Mikasa*
Designer — Bob Paganucci

6.
Client — *Physicians News Network*
Designer — Bob Paganucci

7.
Client — *Waters Corporation*
Designer — Theresa O'Toole

8.
Client — *Foth & Van Dyke*
Designer — Daniel Green

9.
Client — *Z Typography*

10.
Client — *Independent Weatherproofing Consultants, LLC*
Designer — Stephen Allen

11.
Client — *The Spangler Design Team*
Creative Director — Mark Spangler
Artist — Jeff Spry

12.
Client — *Pottery Barn*

13.
Client — *Minnesota Technology, Inc.*
Creative Director — Mark Spangler
Designer — Jeff Spry

14.
Client — *GE Capital*
Art Director — Julia Wyant
Designers — Kristin Kiger, Deborah Davis

15.
Client — *NuAire*
Creative Director — Mark Spangler
Artist — Laura Bartley

16.
Client — *Tech-Pro Inc.*
Designer — Bob Paganucci

17.
Client — *IBM*
Designer — Bob Paganucci

1.

2.

7.

3.

4.

5.

6.

8.

9.

10.

372

11.

12.

13.

14.

15.

16

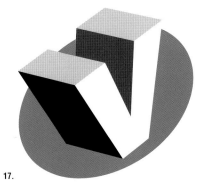

17.

1, 2, 4, 6, 8, 11, 12-15
Design Firm **Paganucci Design, Inc.**
Designer Bob Paganucci
3, 7
Design Firm **By Design**
5
Design Firm **Image Design**
9, 10
Design Firm **Horjus Design**
Designer Peter Horjus
16
Design Firm **Witherspoon Design**
17
Design Firm **Icon Graphics, Inc.**
1.
Client   *IBM*
2.
Client   *IBM*
3.
Client   *D. Chabbott, Inc.*
Designer John Hnath
4.
Client   *Geigy Novartis*
5.
Client   *Masonry Institute/*
          Houston-Galveston
Designer Randy Lynn Witherspoon

6.
Client   *Bell Atlantic*
7.
Client   *Hyde Athletic Industries, Inc.*
Designers John Hnath, Lisa Caputo,
          Elka Raedish
8.
Client   *IBM*
9.
Client   *Byron Pepper*
10.
Client   *The Preference Group*
11.
Client   *ADP*
12.
Client   *Del-Ran*
13.
Client   *Kanes Ltd.*
14.
Client   *SUNY*
15.
Client   *Mikasa*
16.
Client   *O'Connor Company Inc.*
Designer Randi Lynn Witherspoon
17.
Client   *Veritas Technology Inc.*

greenville avenue
Bar and Grill
DALLAS, TEXAS
EST. 1935

1.

OMNIMEDIA
Opening Minds Everywhere

2.

3.

WARNER
MUSIC
GROUP

4.

Matson

5.

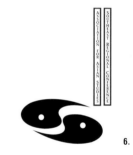

6.

7.

Nacca & Company
CERTIFIED PUBLIC ACCOUNTANTS

8.

9.

10.

374

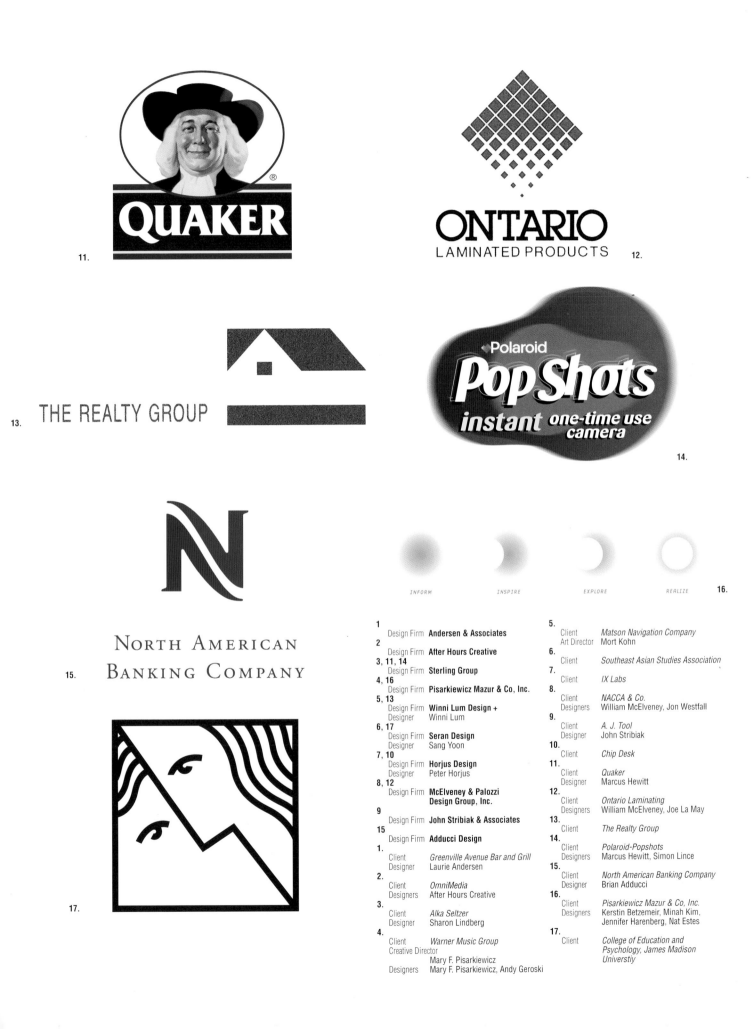

QUAKER

11.

ONTARIO
LAMINATED PRODUCTS

12.

THE REALTY GROUP

13.

Polaroid
Pop Shots
instant one-time use camera

14.

N

NORTH AMERICAN
BANKING COMPANY

15.

INFORM   *INSPIRE*   *EXPLORE*   *REALIZE*   16.

17.

1
Design Firm **Andersen & Associates**
2
Design Firm **After Hours Creative**
3, 11, 14
Design Firm **Sterling Group**
4, 16
Design Firm **Pisarkiewicz Mazur & Co, Inc.**
5, 13
Design Firm **Winni Lum Design +**
Designer Winni Lum
6, 17
Design Firm **Seran Design**
Designer Sang Yoon
7, 10
Design Firm **Horjus Design**
Designer Peter Horjus
8, 12
Design Firm **McElveney & Palozzi Design Group, Inc.**
9
Design Firm **John Stribiak & Associates**
15
Design Firm **Adducci Design**

1.
Client   *Greenville Avenue Bar and Grill*
Designer Laurie Andersen
2.
Client   *OmniMedia*
Designers After Hours Creative
3.
Client   *Alka Seltzer*
Designer Sharon Lindberg
4.
Client   *Warner Music Group*
Creative Director
          Mary F. Pisarkiewicz
Designers Mary F. Pisarkiewicz, Andy Geroski

5.
Client   *Matson Navigation Company*
Art Director Mort Kohn
6.
Client   *Southeast Asian Studies Association*
7.
Client   *IX Labs*
8.
Client   *NACCA & Co.*
Designers William McElveney, Jon Westfall
9.
Client   *A. J. Tool*
Designer John Stribiak
10.
Client   *Chip Desk*
11.
Client   *Quaker*
Designer Marcus Hewitt
12.
Client   *Ontario Laminating*
Designers William McElveney, Joe La May
13.
Client   *The Realty Group*
14.
Client   *Polaroid-Popshots*
Designers Marcus Hewitt, Simon Lince
15.
Client   *North American Banking Company*
Designer Brian Adducci
16.
Client   *Pisarkiewicz Mazur & Co, Inc.*
Designers Kerstin Betzemeir, Minah Kim,
          Jennifer Harenberg, Nat Estes
17.
Client   *College of Education and
          Psychology, James Madison
          Universtiy*

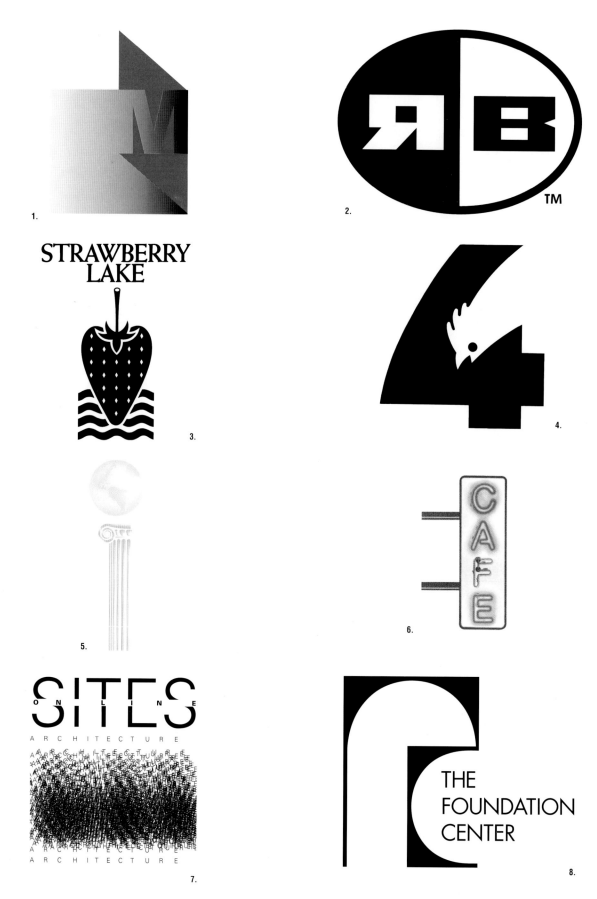

1.

2.

STRAWBERRY
LAKE

3.

4.

5.

C
A
F
E

6.

SITES
O N L I N E
A R C H I T E C T U R E

7.

THE
FOUNDATION
CENTER

8.

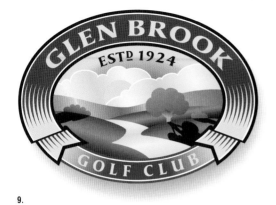

9.

ANDERSEN
& ASSOCIATES

10.

11.

BULLSEYE
DATABASE MARKETING

12.

STARSTREAM
COMMUNICATIONS

14.

13.

∞ INFINITI.
UNIVERSITY
TOTAL | OWNERSHIP EXPERIENCE

15.

1.

2.

3.

4.

5.

6.

7.

8.

9.

10.

11.

12.

MILD LAGER

13.

14.

15.

(all)
Design Firm **Mike Salisbury Communications**
1.
| Client | MCM |
| Designer | Mike Salisbury |

2.
| Client | Rolling Stone |
| Designers | Mike Salisbury, Jim Wood |

3.
| Client | MCD |
| Designer | Mike Salisbury |

4.
| Client | Rage Magazine |
| Designers | Mike Salisbury, Mary Evelyn McGoush |

5.
| Client | Disney |
| Designer | Mike Salisbury |

6.
| Client | Universal Pictures |
| Designers | Mike Salisbury, Dwight Smith |

7.
| Client | Hasbro |
| Designer | Mike Salisbury |

8.
| Client | Birdwell Beach Britches |
| Designer | Mike Salisbury |

9.
| Client | 20th Century Fox |
| Designer | Mike Salisbury |

10.
| Client | Universal Pictures |
| Designers | Mike Salisbury, Tim Martin |

11.
| Client | Mike Salisbury Communications |
| Designers | Mike Salisbury, Robert Grossman |

12.
| Designers | Mike Salisbury, Terry Lamb |

13.
| Client | Kirin Beer |
| Designers | Mike Salisbury, Terry Lamb |

14.
| Client | Universal Pictures |
| Designers | Mike Salisbury, Charlie White, Dave Willardten |

15.
| Client | Gordon & Smith |
| Designer | Mike Salisbury |

1.

2.

3.

4.

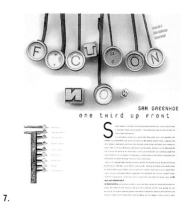

5.

6.

7.

8.

1-3			5.		
Design Firm	**arismendi KNOX, Ltd.**		Client	*Harry's Bar*	
Designers	Susan K. Hodges, Rafael A. Holguín		Designer	Mike Salisbury	
4-8			6.		
Design Firm	**Mike Salisbury Communications**		Client	*Universal Pictures*	
1.			Designer	Mike Salisbury	
Client	*Calidad A Tiempo S. A.*		7.		
2.			Client	*Frances Coppolu*	
Client	*Patchouli Esencias Naturales*		Designers	Mike Salisbury,	
3.				Mary Evelyn McGoush	
Client	*Paloma Promotions & Advertising*		8.		
4.			Client	*Paramount Pictures*	
Client	*Universal Pictures*		Designers	Mike Salisbury, Dave Parmley	
Designers	Mike Salisbury, Terry Lamb				